HUMAN RESOURCE MANAGEMENT

DIBIN SEKHARAN

ISBN 979-888530608-9

This book is dedicated to the M.com students of M.G. University and other management students who want to know more about Human Reource Management.

Contents

Foreword

This book is designed for management students interested in the conceptual background and content that is essential for understanding the relevant issues in human resource management (HRM). It emphasizes a general management approach to HRM to meet the challenges which organizations face in using their human resources effectively. It is structured around key terms stressing the need for proactive HRM to accomplish a competitive edge, and discusses in detail several changes that have taken place in the field of people management especially over the last two decades. It also embodies several old concepts as they provide a sound historical background to understand the new version of personnel management and industrial relations, that is, HRM.

Preface

The last decade has been an interesting period of change and survival for businesses. The worst economic recession in over 50 years forced many companies to rethink the way they did business. More recently, recovery from the recession has presented organizations with a number of different opportunities and threats. Only the best companies survive and thrive in such trying times. But what makes some companies more successful than others? What gives organizations an advantage over their competitors? One answer emphasizes the benefit of having the right people as members of the organization. It is often said that "the people make the place," which tells us that employees are the most important asset of any organization. Practices that help obtain and motivate employees are the core focus of human resource management, which is the field of study presented in this textbook.

As you read this book, we hope you will agree that human resource management is an exciting field of study. In order to make ideas and concepts come to life, we include a number of examples from real companies that illustrate how effective human resource management is helping companies achieve success. Each chapter explains how an organization can increase its effectiveness by improving its processes for hiring and motivating top-performing employees. We also specifically link human resource practices to competitive strategies.

Acknowledgements

It is with a sense of utmost gratitude that i acknowledge my indebtedness to all those who supported and encouraged me in this endeavour. Words fail to express my deep sense of gratitude to Mrs Haritha Dibin, who stood with me in this venture as my backbone, the god almighty and last but not least the publishing agency notion press, who has helped me to bring out this book in a short span of time.

Prologue

Since mid 1980's Human Resource Management (HRM) has gained acceptance in both academic and commercial circle. HRM is a multidisciplinary organizational function that draws theories and ideas from various fields such as management, psychology, sociology and economics. There is no best way to manage people and no manager has formulated how people can be managed effectively, because people are complex beings with complex needs. Effective HRM depends very much on the causes and conditions that an organizational setting would provide. Any Organization has three basic components, People, Purpose, and Structure.

Syllabus

MODULE-1 Human resource management –introduction-nature-features-scopeobjectives-importance-functions-managerial and operative functions of personal management Vs human resource management-qualification and qualities of human resource manager-evolution and growth of HRM in India- (15 Hrs)

MODULE-2 Human resource planning-concept-objectives and importance process-limitations-job analysis. Recruitment-concept-sources-methods and techniques of man power recruitment-characteristics of a good recruitment policy-principles of recruitment-factors affecting recruitment. Selection-concept and procedures-placement and induction. (20 Hrs)

MODULE-3 HRD-concept-objectives-needs-significance-principles of HRD, qualities of an HRD manager. (15 Hrs)

MODULE-4 Motivation-meaning-objective-types of motivation-management techniques to improve motivation-employee morale and productivity nature and significance of morale-factors influencing morale-concepts and significance of productivity-factors influencing productivity. Performance appraisal- meaning purpose-all methods of performance appraisal. (20 Hrs)

MODULE-5 Leadership styles-theories of leadership styles-managerial grid contingency theory-theory X and Y-situational theory-path goal theory-leader participation model-leader member exchange theory-3 D model of leadership-lickert's four system of management charismatic leadership theory-transformational leadership theory social learning approach. (20 Hrs)

CHAPTER ONE

Introduction

Human Resource Management (HRM) is an operation in companies designed to maximize employee performance in order to meet the employer's strategic goals and objectives. More precisely, HRM focuses on management of people within companies, emphasizing on policies and systems.

In short, HRM is the process of recruiting, selecting employees, providing proper orientation and induction, imparting proper training and developing skills.

HRM also includes employee assessment like performance appraisal, facilitating proper compensation and benefits, encouragement, maintaining proper relations with labour and with trade unions, and taking care of employee safety, welfare and health by complying with labour laws of the state or country concerned.

Scope of HRM

The scope of HRM is very wide. It consists of all the functions that come under the banner of human resource management. The different functions are as follows –

Human Resources Planning

It is the process by which a company identifies how many positions are vacant and whether the company has excess staff or shortage of staff and subsequently deals with this need of excess or shortage.

Job Analysis Design

Job analysis can be defined as the process of noticing and regulating in detail the particular job duties and requirements and the relative importance of these duties for a given job.

Job analysis design is a process of designing jobs where evaluations are made regarding the data collected on a job. It gives an elaborate description about each and every job in the company.

Recruitment and Selection

With respect to the information collected from job analysis, the company prepares advertisements and publishes them on various social media platforms. This is known as recruitment.

A number of applications are received after the advertisement is presented, interviews are conducted and the deserving employees are selected. Thus, recruitment and selection is yet another essential area of HRM.

Orientation and Induction

After the employees are selected, an induction or orientation program is organized. The employees are updated about the background of the company as well as culture, values, and work ethics of the company and they are also introduced to the other employees.

Training and Development

Employees have to undergo a training program, which assists them to put up a better performance on the job. Sometimes, training is also conducted for currently working experienced staff so as to help them improve their skills further. This is known as refresher training.

Performance Appraisal

After the employees have put in around 1 year of service, performance appraisal is organized in order to check their performance. On the basis of these appraisals, future promotions, incentives, and increments in salary are decided.

Compensation Planning and Remuneration

Under compensation planning and remuneration, various rules and regulations regarding compensation and related aspects are taken care of. It is the duty of the HR department to look into remuneration and compensation planning.

NATURE OF HUMAN RESOURCE MANAGEMENT

The emergence of human resource management can be attributed to the writings of the human relationists who attached great significance to the human factor. Lawrence Appley remarked, Management is personnel administration‖. This view is partially true as management is concerned with the efficient and effective use of both human as well as non-human resources. Thus, human resource management is only a part of the management process. At the same time, it must be recognised that human resource management is inherent in the process of management. This function is performed by all the managers. A manager to get the best of his people, must undertake the basic responsibility of selecting people who will work under him and to help develop, motivate and guide them. However, he can take the help of the specialised services of the personnel department in discharging this responsibility.

The nature of the human resource management has been highlighted in its following features:

1. **Inherent Part of Management:** Human resource management is inherent in the process of management. This function is performed by all the managers throughout the organisation rather that by the personnel department only. If a manager is to get the best of his people, he must undertake the basic responsibility of selecting people

who will work under him.

2. **Pervasive Function:** Human Resource Management is a pervasive function of management. It is performed by all managers at various levels in the organisation. It is not a responsibility that a manager can leave completely to someone else. However, he may secure advice and help in managing people from experts who have special competence in personnel management and industrial relations.
3. **Basic to all Functional Areas:** Human Resource Management permeates all the functional area of management such as production management, financial management, and marketing management. That is every manager from top to bottom, working in any department has to perform the personnel functions.
4. **People Centered:** Human Resource Management is people centered and is relevant in all types of organisations. It is concerned with all categories of personnel from top to the bottom of the organisation. The broad classification of personnel in an industrial enterprise may be as follows: (I) Blue-collar workers (i.e., those working on machines and engaged in loading, unloading etc.) and white-collar workers (i.e., clerical employees), (ii) Managerial and non-managerial personnel, (iii) Professionals (such as Chartered Accountant, Company Secretary, Lawyer, etc.) and non- professional personnel.
5. **Personnel Activities or Functions:** Human Resource Management involves several functions concerned with the management of people at work. It includes manpower planning, employment, placement, training, appraisal and compensation of employees. For the performance of these activities efficiently, a separate department known as Personnel Department is created in most of the organisations.
6. **Continuous Process:** Human Resource Management is not a _one shot 'function. It must be performed continuously if the organisational objectives are to be achieved smoothly.
7. **Based on Human Relations:** Human Resource Management is concerned with the motivation of human resources in the organisation. The human beings can't be dealt with like physical factors of production. Every person has different needs, perceptions and expectations. The managers should give due attention to these factors. They require human relations skills to deal with the people at work. Human relations skills are also required in training performance appraisal, transfer and promotion of subordinates.

Features of Human Resource Management (HRM)

Feature # 1. Universal Force:

HRM is universal in nature; it is present in all organizations and is applicable at all levels of the management in an organization. As a matter of fact, HRM is concerned and closely associated with the strategic decision-making process of the organization involving all departments and functions in the organization. Thus, even for a budding SME entrepreneur knowledge of HRM would be instrumental for successfully managing his people without having any formal HR systems in his organization.

Feature # 2. Decision Oriented:

HRM emphasizes on decisions, rather than on record keeping, written procedures or rules, which had long been the responsibilities of traditional personnel management practices. These decisions might involve those with respect to performance improvement through further training, or a promotion decision based on satisfactory performance by an employee.

Feature # 3. Focus on Individual Needs and Aspirations:

HRM emphasizes on identifying the individual needs and aspirations of an individual employee on the basis of through analysis of their capabilities and future potential. Thus, it makes an attempt to help these individuals to further develop their potential and encourage them to give their best to the organization.

Thus, for a B School faculty, his/her promotions to higher designations might well be related to contributions in research and development or management consultancy and such decisions would be at the discretion of the management of these institutes depending on the nature and framework used to assess the performance of the faculties.

Feature # 4. Employee Oriented:

HRM is concerned about people. Conventionally HRM authors have denied concern for people with employees at work, both as individuals, as well as in groups and teams. But in today's highly competitive business perspective, concern for people has a wider domain conceptually.

It mainly deals and revolves around the capabilities of the people rather than the individual. Thus, the paradigm shift had been from assigning people on allotted tasks to utilize knowledge and human capabilities for higher performance outcomes.

Feature # 5. Development and Growth Oriented:

Development had been long conceptualized as an initiative taken by an organization to acquire better work-related skills and behaviours. In the context where organizations are emphasizing more upon sharing and developing knowledge, the concept of development attains a wider or broader meaning in terms of realizing the capabilities of people/rather knowledge workers.

Behavioural scientists have argued that holistic development of people can be made instrumental if the former is coupled with reinforcement strategies ensuring the acquisition of the desired behaviour and capabilities among people. The reward and incentive structures of organizations are needed to be fine-tuned along with the development-oriented initiatives taken by the organization.

Feature # 6. Binding Force of an Organization:

HRM has the additional responsibility of treating their employees as the "internal customers" of the organization. In this perspective HR professionals need to assume the role of experts (internal business consultants) in other functional domains of their organization like logistics, finance, supply chain management, total quality management, marketing and corporate relations so as to facilitate organizational effectiveness.

Feature # 7. Strategic Implication:

In the perspective of today's highly competitive business environment, HRM should assume the role of the strategic decision-making process in the organization. HR professionals in this regard need to assume the responsibility of being the strategic partners of the business and helping the organization to successfully achieve their business objectives by aligning people to the strategic goals of the organization.

Feature # 8. Support Functions:

The HR function of an organization is service oriented. HR executives provide support services to the line managers working in other departments not only just accomplish their administrative or HR-related work more effectively, they so provide consultation as internal consultants and extend "subject-matter-expert (SME)" help and assistances whenever required. HR activities like talent tracking, reward management are examples of the service function.

Feature # 9. Multi-Disciplinary Nature:

HRM is a multi-disciplinary practice drawing the knowledge and inputs drawn from various disciplines and studies like those of psychology, sociology, anthropology, political science, economics, quantitative techniques and statistical applications, econometrics, ergonomics (Quality of life and work environment designing), financial concepts (Human resource accounting and HR-audit) etc. The multi-disciplinary aspect of HR function, helps HR professionals assume the role of strategic partners as well as internal consultants of the organization.

Feature # 10. Ongoing and Forward-Looking Nature:

HRM is an ongoing process that starts at the strategic level in the organization and pervades into each and every functional domain of the organization. Today's HR practices are mostly forward looking and they constantly take into consideration the future needs and requirements of the business.

Width of Human Resourse Management

Human resources are undoubtedly the key resources in an organization, the easiest and the most difficult to manage! The objectives of the HRM span right from the manpower needs assessment to management and retention of the same. To this effect Human resource management is responsible for effective designing and implementation of various policies, procedures and programs. It is all about developing and managing knowledge, skills, creativity, aptitude and talent and using them optimally.

Human Resource Management is not just limited to manage and optimally exploit human intellect. It also focuses on managing physical and emotional capital of employees. Considering the intricacies involved, the scope of HRM is widening with every passing day. It covers but is not limited to HR planning, hiring (recruitment and selection), training and development, payroll management, rewards and recognitions, Industrial relations, grievance handling, legal procedures etc. In other words, we can say that it's about developing and managing harmonious relationships at workplace and striking a balance between organizational goals and individual goals.

The scope of HRM is extensive and far-reaching. Therefore, it is very difficult to define it concisely. However, we may classify the same under following heads:

- **HRM in Personnel Management:** This is typically direct manpower management that involves manpower planning, hiring (recruitment and selection), training and development, induction and orientation, transfer, promotion, compensation, layoff and retrenchment, employee productivity. The overall objective here is to ascertain individual growth, development and effectiveness which indirectly contribute to organizational development.

It also includes performance appraisal, developing new skills, disbursement of wages, incentives, allowances, traveling policies and procedures and other related courses of actions.

- **HRM in Employee Welfare:** This particular aspect of HRM deals with working conditions and amenities at workplace. This includes a wide array of responsibilities and services such as safety services, health services, welfare funds, social security and medical services. It also covers appointment of safety officers, making the environment worth working, eliminating workplace hazards, support by top management, job safety, safeguarding machinery, cleanliness, proper ventilation and lighting, sanitation, medical care, sickness benefits, employment injury benefits, personal injury benefits, maternity benefits, unemployment benefits and family benefits.

It also relates to supervision, employee counselling, establishing harmonious relationships with employees, education and training. Employee welfare is about determining employees' real needs and fulfilling them with active participation of both management and employees. In addition to this, it also takes care of canteen facilities, crèches, rest and lunch rooms, housing, transport, medical assistance, education, health and safety, recreation facilities, etc.

- **HRM in Industrial Relations:** Since it is a highly sensitive area, it needs careful interactions with labour or employee unions, addressing their grievances and settling the disputes effectively in order to maintain peace and harmony in the organization. It is the art and science of understanding the employment (union-management) relations, joint consultation, disciplinary procedures, solving problems with mutual efforts, understanding human behaviour and maintaining work relations, collective bargaining and settlement of disputes.

The main aim is to safeguarding the interest of employees by securing the highest level of understanding to the extent that does not leave a negative impact on organization. It is about establishing, growing and promoting industrial democracy to safeguard the interests of both employees and management.

Objectives of HRM

Below are 8 main HRM objectives with in-depth elaboration respectively:

- **Achieve organisational goals**
- **Work culture**
- **Team integration**
- **Training and Development**
- **Employee motivation**
- **Workforce empowerment**
- **Retention**
- **Data and compliance**

Achieve organisational goals

HRM function starts here. One major HRM objective is to fulfil organisational goals. Utilizing human resource to achieve business requirements and goals is very important for an effective HRM.

Organisational objectives include workforce handling, staff requirements like hiring and onboarding, payroll management and retirement. To succeed at organisational objective, HR requires efficient planning and execution. Without a set parameter for goals and mission and resources, HRM is incomplete. After you know your resources and planning at place, achieving HRM objective is not so difficult.

Some more objectives are explained further.

Work culture

When it comes to handling HRM effectively and following objectives, employee and work environment are the prior factors. Work culture plays an important role in defining HRM and business performance.

An HR manager needs to be active while calling for strategies to foster better work culture. Automated activities like leave approvals, reimbursement request acknowledgement, etc. can help you. Quick operations and empowerment to employees help in creative positive vibes at workplace. Developing and maintaining healthy and transparent relations among team members and teams contribute to building a good example of work culture. Adopting right solutions like employment management software can solve more than half of your job.

Small steps like short and sound onboarding process can help build good image of workplace.

Team Integration

One of the prime roles and objectives of HRM is to make sure team co-ordinate efficiently. Easy communication is the need for teams at an enterprise. An HR here must ensure a tool to assist in making the integration easier and smooth.

Proper connect between individuals is a must to ensure productivity. To make the HR management a success, you need to search better integration portals to make data availability easier for people. Functional objectives like team integration are to produce streamlined operations and tasks.

With right tool like self-service portal can bring employees closer to HR folks.

Training and Development

Workforce being effective and performing are two important and basic elements to work upon for achieving your basic objectives at an organisation. With proper training and providing future opportunities, employees feel safe and organised.

Effective employment is highly dependent upon the training practices. Providing opportunities to employees is one great step to ensure workforce management.

There might be difficulties such as planning, scheduling, training sessions, and evaluation of each on-boards. To lessen the pain, solution like training management software can help you with auto-reminders, easy scheduler, reporting, and tracking capability. The HR manager can ensure effective training practice at firm.

Employee Motivation

The prime objective of an HR folk is to keep things on right path. Keep distractions and negative vibes away. For this the employees need to be attended and kept motivated throughout.

Give powers to them. Take their views on things. Involve them into weekly meets or decisions. Even if it is a fresher, let them join. Keep the morale always high. Employee recognition like yearly appraisal based on their performance can to help.

Automated feedback system for performance appraisal management can keep your employees motivated and ensure productivity throughout service. When the employees are satisfied and fulfilled, nothing else can prevent you from losing your objectives and goals.

Workforce empowerment

Talking about employee motivation, nothing can work better than empowering them. Empowering them with tools like ESS (employee self-service) portal can help save HR efforts too.

With the portal, employees can themselves apply for approvals and track them through their mobile phone. Be it leave request, generating payslip, checking PF account, remaining leaves, upcoming holidays, manager details, or anything, HR intervention is least required. Now, you no more need to knock on HR's desk for small queries.

Retention

Providing leadership qualities and opportunities, healthy working area, and employee retention are some prime objectives and deliverables of HR manager. Keeping employees retained and motivated needs to be a top priority for HRM.

Other than employee hiring, onboarding, and training cycle, keeping the employees retained for long is the biggest challenge AKA objective of the HR people. It often occurs that employees leave the organisation within 2 months of onboarding. It can be due to ineffective training management or rough hiring process.

Employee experience needs to be carefully attended. Keeping your employees retained can help maintain good state of employee turnover. To keep it stable, the HR manager needs to learn the best retention tips for business.

Data and compliance

Functional and organisational objectives also include managing company/ employee data and managing compliances. Managing payroll compliances and keeping the company out of any penalties or fine is huge challenge for HR people and managers.

Even a small error or miscalculation can owe you huge penalties and even may lose respect. When committing to tasks like employment and payroll, you need to be careful about laws and regulations. Objective here is to keep any unwanted claims at bay for smooth functioning.

Automated software like HRMS system can help you keep errors at side and leave no window for owing any penalty from IRS. It is the responsibility of HR to follow IRS guidelines and standards for effective employment at company. Stay assured with all the legalities.

FUNCTIONS OF HUMAN RESOURCE MANAGEMENT

1) Human resource planning

The principal function of HR is to know the future needs of the company. What sort of individuals does the company need, and how many? Understanding this will shape the recruitment, determination, execution of the executives, learning & development, and all other functions of HRM.

2) Recruitment

The second function of HR includes recruiting people to work for the organization and selecting the best suitors. Recruiting individuals generally begins with an employer brand. Being an alluring employer has many advantages and vice versa. For instance, a tobacco business that battles to pull in talent because of its tainted reputation. With a reliable employer brand and the privilege of sourcing policies, you're almost halfway there. When candidates apply, the selection process is an HR's instrument to pick the best qualified and most potential candidates.

3) Performance management

Performance management is essential in ensuring that workers stay productive and engaged. Good performance management includes sound leadership, clear goal-setting, and welcoming feedback. Performance management tools include the (bi)annual performance evaluation, in which their manager reviews the performance of the employee. It also incorporates 360-degree feedback tools in which peers, directors, subordinates, and even clients evaluate the employee's performance. Performance management is additionally an instrument to close the gap between the workforce you have today and the one you will need tomorrow. Probably the ideal approach to build your future workforce is through Learning & Development (L&D). Performance management is one of the vital functions of the HR department.

4) Learning & development

Empowering representatives to build the skills they require in the future is one of the fundamental functions of HRM. Every organization understands the value of investing in the reskilling of its employees. It is one of the vital functions of the HR department to lead these efforts in the right direction.

5) Career planning

One of the vital functions of HRM includes career planning, guidance, and growth for employees. Guiding employees about how their aspirations can align with the organization's objectives helps to engage and retain them.

6) Information sharing

One of the essential functions of human resource management is sharing information with employees; this can be through a newsletter to keep everyone up to date with the latest news. It likewise involves safety procedures, announcements of layoffs, mergers, or acquisition, or any other significant occasion applicable for employees. Clear, straightforward, and ideal information sharing is critical in building and keeping up help and successful organizational change.

7) Rewards & recognitions

Recognition & rewards, one of the many functions of HRM, is to appreciate employees' efforts and to sustain notable talent. Rewards and recognition make employees feel worthy of their work as the appreciation serves as motivation. They can be financial or non-monetary rewards.

8) Compensation & benefits

This function of HR requires continual observation of industry pay benchmarks and keeping up with the industry standards, including new and variable payment parameters in salary, simple pay expectations, and faster processes. Money is the prime motivation that drives individuals to work. Nonetheless, to retain individuals, this function is very important.

9) Industrial relations

Another crucial function of HR is managing and cultivating relationships with labor unions, other forums, and their members.

10) Policy formulation

Policies are the backbone functions of Human Resource Management. An organization needs policies that are tried and tested as much as it needs policies that are more up to date and sensitive. A reasonable and well-defined policy framework structure covers all the minute aspects of a company and its operations. Policies can control activities like better participation, standardized methods, procedures & implementation, and proper communication, to name a few.

11) Health and safety

Devising and implementing health and safety regulations are one of the significant functions of HRM.

12) Personal well-being

Supporting and taking care of employees when they're having personal problems that affect their performance is a key function of HR. Emotional well-being is about helping employees when circumstances don't go as planned.

13) Employee engagement

Employee engagement, as one of the essential functions of human resource management, has gained much attention over recent years affecting employee turnover positively to a considerable extent. Furthermore, introducing exciting employee engagement initiatives can acquire new and brilliant talent in the company. Organizations are putting significant sums in employee engagement to convince employees that they matter.

14) Compliance

As an HR professional, seeing that your organization is complying with labor laws is one of the crucial functions of HR. The HR management department understands these legal concerns and ensures that the employcc and the organization are protected. Compliance comprises the estimation of leave, payroll legalization, govt. and tax reporting, etc.

15) Administrative responsibilities

One of the crucial functions of human resource management includes administrative responsibilities. Operations like relocations, further upskilling, promotions, illness, leaves, and many more come under this function.

Importance of HRM

The Importance of HRM must be viewed through of overall strategic goals for the organization instead of a standalone tint that takes a unit based or a micro approach. The idea here is to adopt a holistic perspective towards HRM that ensures that there are no piecemeal strategies and the HRM policy enmeshes itself fully with those of the organizational goals.HRM becomes significant for business organization due to the following reasons.

The importance of HRM are:

1. **Objective** :-

HRM helps a company to achieve its objective from time to time by creating a positive attitude among workers. Reducing wastage and making maximum use of resources etc.

2. **Facilitates professional growth** :-

Due to proper HR policies employees are trained well and this makes them ready for future promotions. Their talent can be utilized not only in the company in which they are currently working but also in other companies which the employees may join in the future.

3. **Better relations between union and management** :-

Healthy HRM practices can help the organization to maintain co-ordinal relationship with the unions. Union members start realizing that the company is also interested in the workers and will not go against them therefore chances of going on strike are greatly reduced.

4. **Helps an individual to work in a team/group** :-

Effective HR practices teach individuals team work and adjustment. The individuals are now very comfortable while working in team thus team work improves.

5. **Identifies person for the future** :-

Since employees are constantly trained, they are ready to meet the job requirements. The company is also able to identify potential employees who can be promoted in the future for the top level jobs. Thus one of the advantages of HRM is preparing people for the future.

6. **Allocating the jobs to the right person** :-

If proper recruitment and selection methods are followed, the company will be able to select the right people for the right job. When this happens the number of people leaving the job will reduce as the will be satisfied with their job leading to decrease in labor turnover.

7. **Improves the economy** :

Effective HR practices lead to higher profits and better performance by companies due to this the company achieves a chance to enter into new business and start new ventured thus industrial development increases and the economy improves.

Functions of Personnel Management

1. Managerial Functions
2. Operative Functions

1. Managerial Functions:

The Managerial functions of a personnel manager involve POSDCORB (Luther Gullick) i.e., Planning, organisation, staffing, directing, coordinating, reporting and budgeting of those who actually perform the operative functions of the Personnel Department.

The following are the managerial functions (viz. planning, organising, directing and controlling) performed by a personnel department:

A. Personnel Planning:

Planning lays down a pre-determined course to do something such as what to do, how to do, where to do, who is to do etc. A personnel manager plans in advance the trend in wages, labour market, union demands etc. Through planning, most of the future problems can be anticipated.

B. Organising:

According to J.C. Massic, "An organisation is a structure, a framework and a process by which a co-operative group of human being allocates its task among its members, identifies relationships and integrates its activities towards common objectives." The personnel manager has to design the structure of relationships among jobs, personnel and physical factors so that the objectives of the enterprise are achieved.

C .Directing:

This function relates to guidance and stimulation of the subordinates at all levels. The personnel manager directs and motivates the employees of his department so that they work willingly and effectively for the achievement of organisational goals,

D. Controlling:

A personnel manager has to constantly watch whether there is any deviation from the planned path. Controlling is concerned with remedial actions. Continuous monitoring of the personnel policies relating to training, labour turnover, wage payments, interviewing new and separated employees etc., is the backbone of controlling.

If deviations are unavoidable, corrective action can be planned in advance. Controlling helps the personnel manager to evaluate the performance of employees of the personnel department so far as the operating functions are concerned.

2. Operative Functions:

The operative functions of the Personnel Department are also called service functions. These include.

(a) Procurement function
(b) Development
(c) Promotion, transfer and termination function
(d) Compensation function
(e) Welfare function
(f) Collective bargaining function

(g) Miscellaneous functions.

These functions of the personnel Department are discussed below:

(1) Procurement:

It includes:

(a) Recruitment i.e., tapping the possible sources from where prospective labour supply will come.

(b) Getting information regarding prevailing wage rates and job requirements.

(c) Selecting the best candidate by following a systematic selection procedure.

(d) Maintaining the records of employees.

(e) Introducing the new employee to the officers of the other departments such as Security Officer, Time Keeper, and Cashier etc.

(2) Training or Development Function:

The training of the new employees and also of those who are being promoted is the crucial function of Personnel Department. A training programme is devised for this purpose. The training increases the skills and abilities of the employees.

The various aspects of training are:

(a) Training to new employees, instructors and supervisors.

(b) Training in safety equipments and various policies of companies.

(c) Training through improvement of education such as evening classes, films, Entertainment programmes etc.

(d) Encouraging employees to give suggestions.

(3) Promotion, Transfer and Termination:

The performance of the employees is evaluated for the purpose of taking decisions concerning the employment. Merit rating is undertaken for evaluation of the performance of the employees.

The functions of the Personnel Department in this regard are given below:

(a) To lay down a promotion policy.

(b) To formulate policies regarding transfer and termination.

(c) Analysis of voluntary separations and knowing the possible causes of such separations.

(4) Compensation:

The employees should get adequate and equitable remuneration for the work being done by them.

The functions of the Personnel Department concerned with fixation of fair wages are:

(a) To evaluate jobs and determine their worth in terms of money.

(b) To collaborate with those who formulate wage plans.

(c) To assist in formulation of policies regarding pension plans, profit sharing programmes, non-monetary benefits, etc.

(d) To compare the wages of the enterprise with the industry and remove inconsistencies, if any.

(5) Welfare Activities:

These activities relate to physical and social well-being of the employees and include:

(a) Provision of medical facilities such as first aid, dispensaries, etc.

(b) Suggesting ways and means by which accidents can be eliminated or minimised.

(c) To make provisions for restaurants and other recreational facilities.

(d) To apply the labour laws effectively.

(e) To publish a plant magazine.

(6) Collective Bargaining:

It includes:

(a) To assist in the negotiations which are held with the union leaders

(b) To know the grievances of employees and following their problems properly.

(7) Miscellaneous:

(a) To advise the line managers regarding administration of personnel policies.

(b) To secure co-ordination of all personnel activities.

(c) To have an effective communication system.

(d) To provide good working conditions.

QUALIFICATION AND QUALITIES OF HUMAN RESOURCE MANAGER

The functions of personnel management vary from organization to organization both in nature and degree. So, the qualifications required of a personnel manager differ from organization to organization depending on its nature, size, location etc. However, the qualification and qualities which will be applicable in general can be summarized as follows:

Personal Attributes:

The personnel manager, as in case of any other manager, must have initiative, resourcefulness, depth of perception, maturity in judgment and analytical ability. Freedom from bias would enable the personnel manager to take an objectives view of both of management and workers. He must thus have intellectual integrity. Moreover, the personnel manager should be thorough will labor laws. An understanding of human behavior is essential to the personnel manager. The personnel manager must be familiar with human needs, wants, hopes and desires, values, aspirations etc., without which adequate motivation is impossible.

The Personnel Manager should also possess other personal attributes like:

1. Intelligence: This includes skills to communicate, articulate, moderate, understand, command over language, mental ability, tact in dealing with people intelligently, ability to draft agreements, policies etc.

2. Educational Skills: Personnel Manager should possess learning and teaching skills as he has to learn and teach employees about the organizational growth, need for and mode of development of individuals etc.

3. Discriminating Skills: Personnel manager should have the ability to discriminate between right and wrong, between the just and unjust, merit and demerit.

4. Executing Skills: The Personnel Manager is expected to execute the management's decisions regarding personnel issues with speed, accuracy and objectivity. He should also be able to streamline the office, set standards of performance, co-ordinate, control etc.

Further, the personnel manager is expected to have leadership qualities: deep faith in human values, empathy with human problems, foreseeing future needs of employees, organization, government, trade unions, society etc.

Experience and Training:

Previous experience is undoubtedly an advantage provided the experience was in an appropriate environment and in the same area. Training in psychological aspects, labor legislations and more specifically in personnel management and general management is an additional benefit. Experience in an enterprise in some other executive capacity can also help towards an appreciation of the general management problems and a practical approach in meeting personnel problems.

Professional Attitude:

Finally, professional attitudes are more necessary particularly in Indian context. The personnel managers, as in the case of other manager is getting professionalized. He should have patience and understanding ability to listen before offering advice. He should have Knowledge of various disciplines like technology, engineering management, sociology, psychology, philosophy, human physiology, economics, commerce, and law. He must be able to couple his social justice with a warm personal interest in people which must be secured by an uncommon degree of common sense.

Qualifications:

Qualifications prescribed for the post of Personnel Manager vary from industry to industry and from State to State. These qualifications have been undergoing several changes from time to time.

In India the qualifications demanded by almost all the companies are M.B.A. with HR specialization or M.A. (Social sciences) from reputed institutes like Institute of Tata Social sciences or Xavier Labor Institute and a few other Institutes. However some organizations internally promote or transfer some competent managers to HR positions to provide growth opportunity. Even reputed companies like L&T, Hindusthan Lever and others have adopted the transfer measure to fill up personnel positions as and when required. Even managers with engineering qualifications from Materials management, Production functions were made Head of HR department in some reputed firms.

It is the competency, personnel handling & negotiating skills that are required more than the qualifications. Labor laws and acts can be briefed by experts in the organization or outside consultants if the manager does not have the specific qualifications which cover the legal aspects.

EVOLUTION OF HRM IN INDIA

India is the largest democracy in the world & one of the oldest human civilizations. The country has a rich history and diverse culture. It is a birthplace of four of the world's major religions and is characterized by a diversity of religious beliefs & practices. India is one of the exciting emerging economies which add 10+ million people to its working force every year. A very efficient HRM system and labour policies are required to handle a huge & diverse country like ours. Let's look at the evolution of Human Resources Management (HRM) in India.

India has a deep-rooted value system which influenced the societies & working institutes. Collective culture has always prioritized values of duty towards family & society. Even the world's first management book "Arthashastra" was written in India around 300 BC which has two major ideologies related to present Human Resources, 1) Public Policy & 2) Administration & Utilization of people. Long back we were aware that the greatest asset of any organization is its people. We can see from the Mauryan period (320 BC to 181 BC) that there were a variety of craftsmen, artists, labourers, etc. who were employed in various activities including mining, metallurgy, forces etc. owned by the state. There used to be appointed officers who used to look after the welfare of the workers. We also see traces of formed unions of craftsmen in the history and few instances mentioning fixed pay for the workers to strengthen job stability.

During the British Era, industrialization took place in India and various labour laws such as "Factories Act", "Workmen's Compensation Act", "Mines Act", "Truck Act" and "Trade Union Act" were enacted. There were few discriminatory policies, however, Indian employers continued to grow on British policies. Initially, line managers used to handle the labour, however with the growing size of the workforce and increasing complexity at work, a separate department which deals with labour matters came into existence, especially in large scale industrial establishments. Few main features of this labour/personnel management department were authoritarian control, strict supervision, provision of some incentives to increase production & emphasis on discipline and general indifference towards human aspects. The progress in the HRM field was continuous before independence and many of our freedom fighters also pressurized employers to improvise their approach towards workers and give due attention to human aspects in their enterprise.

Post-Independence, there was thrust on HRM. Adoption of the Indian constitution, which contains significant clauses related to labour welfare and various human resources angle came into force. Apart from the constitution, there were a series of labour laws and enactments which brought several labour/human resource matters under the domain of state intervention. These labour laws have resulted in the enlargement of the functional areas of personnel management by covering a variety of aspects concerning workers and setting up minimum standards in many of these areas. The requirement of appointing welfare officers in factories and mines of prescribed size reflects the desire of the government to recognize the need for and importance of giving due consideration to human aspects in the industry.

In present times, the Indian industry has emerged stronger and companies across all industries have seen good results. The Indian Industrial Sector, HRM is regulated mainly by the government where multiple laws & policies for workers have to be followed by organizations. In the private sector especially for the global linked organizations, the expectations of the employees are very dynamic & retention of the employees is a challenge. As per the survey results of 2019 (also shown in the graphs as under), average salary increases stands at 9.8% and average annual attrition at 13.1%.

The role of HR is very dynamic in the present Indian scenario. The role has evolved from earlier supporting role of managing payrolls and manpower to a strategic partner in the growth of the business. It's now an integral part of the corporate and now innovative HR practices have also been USP of many companies. Presently HR does the following role in the Indian context –

1. Investing in Talent (i.e., employee experience, Happiness at work & Employee wellness)
2. Bracing for Diversity
3. Greater Emphasis on Employee Development.
4. Use of Technology in HR.
5. Motivating the Workforce
6. Managing People
7. Competency Development
8. Trust Factor
9. Work-life Balance
10. Bridging the demand-supply gap

HRM has started focusing more on development aspects of human resources.

HRM emphasis on a harmonious balance between employee demands & organizational requirements.

Development of HRM in India has now occupied a centre stage and its growing at an apt pace with the industry.

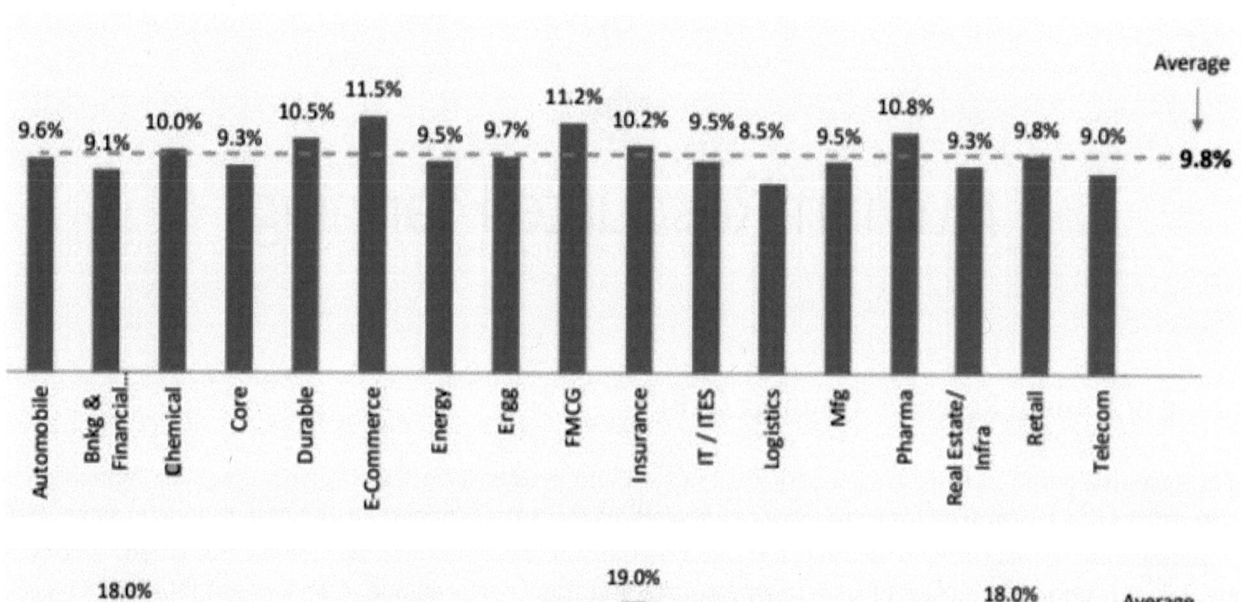
Average
9.6%
9.1%
10.0%
9.3%
10.5%
11.5%
9.5%
9.7%
11.2%
10.2%
9.5%
8.5%
9.5%
10.8%
9.3%
9.8%
9.0%
9.8%
Automobile
Bnkg & Financial...
Chemical
Core
Durable
E-Commerce
Energy
Ergg
FMCG
Insurance
IT / ITES
Logistics
Mfg
Pharma
Real Estate/ Infra
Retail
Telecom

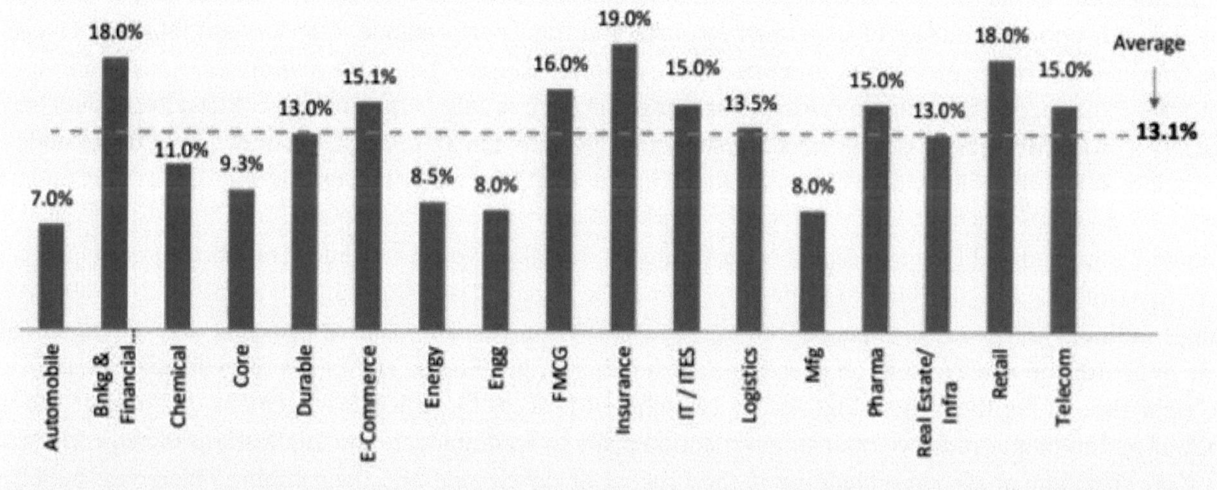
Average
7.0%
18.0%
11.0%
9.3%
13.0%
15.1%
8.5%
8.0%
16.0%
19.0%
15.0%
13.5%
8.0%
15.0%
13.0%
18.0%
15.0%
13.1%
Automobile
Bnkg & Financial...
Chemical
Core
Durable
E-Commerce
Energy
Engg
FMCG
Insurance
IT / ITES
Logistics
Mfg
Pharma
Real Estate/ Infra
Retail
Telecom
HR Trends 2019

HR Trends

CHAPTER TWO

Human Resource Planning

Meaning of Human Resource Planning (HRP)

Human Resource is the most vital factor for the survival and prosperity of the organization. The human resource asset in a firm has the potential to appreciate the value of the firm. Though all the firms buy the same material and machines, the people in a firm make the difference in the final product. So the success of any organization mainly depends upon the quality of its human resource and their performance. Any forward looking management will be concerned with the problem of procuring or developing adequate talent for manning various positions in the organization. The success of a human resource planning process not only helps the organization itself, but also helps the society's prosperity. The losses a firm suffers from inadequate human resource planning and utilization is a loss to the nation. When these individual losses are added up the total losses may be very significant to the economy of a nation.

Human resource may be regarded as the quantitativeand qualitative measurement of labor force required in an organization and planning in relation to manpower may be regarded as establishing objectives to develop human resources in line with broad objectives of the organization. Thus, human resource planning may be expressed as a process by which the management ensures the right number of people and right kind of people, at the right place, at the right time doing the right things. It is a two-phased process by which management can project the future manpower requirements and develop manpower action plans to accommodate the implications of projections. Thus, we can say that human resource planning is the process of developing and determining objectives, policies and programmers that will develop utilize and distribute manpower so as to achieve the goals of the organization.

Definitions of Human Resource Planning

Human Resource Planning is the planning of Human Resources. It is also called manpower planning/ personnel planning/ employment planning. It is only after Human Resource Planning that the Human Resource department can initiate the recruitment and selection process. Therefore Human Resource Planning is a sub-system of organisational planning.

Definitions of Human Resource Planning by eminent authors;

- "Human Resource Planning is a strategy for the acquisition, utilization, improvement and preservation of an organisation's human resource." – Y.C. Moushell
- "Manpower planning is the process by which a firm ensures that it has the right number of people and the right kind of people, at the right places, at the right time, doing things for which they are economically mast useful". – Edwin B. Geisler
- "Human Resource Planning is a process of forecasting an organisation's future demand for human resource and supply of right type of people in right numbers." – J.Chennly.K
- "Human Resource Planning is an integrated approach to perform the planning aspects of the personnel function. It ensures sufficient supply of adequately developed and motivated workforce to perform the required duties and tasks to meet organization's objectives by satisfying the individual needs and goals of organizational members." – Leon C. Megginson
- "A strategy for the acquisition, utilization, improvement, and preservation of human resources of an enterprise. It is a way of dealing with people in a dynamic situation." – Stainer
- "The process of determining manpower requirements and the means for meeting those requirements to carry out the integrated plan of the organization." – Bruce P. Coleman
- "Human Resource Planning as the process by which management determines how the organization should move from its current manpower position to its desired position. Through planning, management strives to have the right number and the right kind of people, at the right places, at the right time, doing right things resulting in maximum long-run benefits both for the organization and for the individual." – Vetter

Features of Human Resource Planning

1. It is future oriented: Human Resource Planning is forward-looking. It involves forecasting the manpower needs for a future period so that adequate and timely provisions may be made to meet the needs.
2. It is a continuous process: Human Resource Planning is a continuous process because the demand and supply of Human Resource keeps fluctuating throughout the year. Human Resource Planning has to be reviewed according to the needs of the organisation and changing environment.
3. Integral part of Corporate Planning: Manpower planning is an integral part of corporate planning because without a corporate plan there can be no manpower planning.

4. Optimum utilization of resources: The basic purpose of Human Resource Planning is to make optimum utilization of organisation's current and future human resources.
5. Both Qualitative and Quantitative aspect: Human Resource Planning considers both the qualitative and quantitative aspects of Human Resource Management, 'Quantitative' meaning the right number of people and 'Qualitative' implying the right quality of manpower required in the organisation.
6. Long term and Short term: Human Resource Planning is both Long-term and short-term in nature. Just like planning which is long-term and short-term depending on the need of the hour, Human Resource Planning keeps long-term goals and short-term goals in view while predicting and forecasting the demand and supply of Human Resource.
7. Involves study of manpower requirement: Human Resource Planning involves the study of manpower availability and the manpower requirement in the organisation.

Significance of Human Resource Planning

The failure in planning and in developing personnel will prove to be a limiting factor in attributing to the organizational objectives. If the number of persons in an organization is less than the number of persons required to carry out the organizational plans, there will be disruptions in the flow of work and the production will also be lowered. But if, on the other hand, some persons are surplus in an organization, they will have to be paid remuneration. The sound personnel policy requires that there should be adequate number of persons of the right type to attain its objectifies. For this the manpower planner should be concerned with the training and the scheduling of the planning of personnel and persuading the management to use the results of manpower planning studies in the conduct of the business. Every industrial or commercial organization has the need of proper system of manpower planning so as to bring efficiency and economy in the organization. Smaller concerns and those with simpler organizations also require human resource planning though at a small scale. Human resource planning can prove to be an important aid to frame the training and development programmes for the personnel because it takes into account the effects of anticipated changes in technology, markets and products on manpower requirements and educational and training programme requirements.

Human resource planning is relatively a difficult task for the personnel management. It is particularly so in business enterprises which are often subject to forces outside their control such as social, political and economical changes. Manpower is a key resource required for the achievement of business objectives. Materials, equipment's, power and other resources can be effectively and efficiently used, only if there is manpower capable of processing them into required goods and services. It takes a long time to develop the manpower of right type to use these resources. Therefore, decisions concerning manpower development must be taken many years in advance. However, management may stick to short periods for rank and file employees, but it will have to concentrate upon the problems of replacing key professional and managerial personnel on a long term basis. In as-much-as many big organizations do prepare long-range forecasts in production, marketing and capital investment, it should not be surprising if it makes long term projections in regard to its personnel. However, human resource plans cannot be rigid or static, they can be modified or adjusted according to the change in the circumstances.

Purposes of Human Resource Planning

The primary function of Personnel planning is to analyze and evaluate the available human resources within the organization. It also determines how to obtain the kinds of needed personnel to staff various organisational positions starting from assembly line workers to chief executives. Smaller companies have assigned the function of HR planning to the human resource department or personnel department. Larger corporations have separate departments for this function. Personnel planning aims at minimization of waste in employing people, lessen uncertainty of current personnel levels and future needs, and eliminate mistakes in staffing pattern. The purpose of Human Resource Planning aims at maintaining the required level of skill by avoiding workforce skill shortages, stopping the profit-eroding effects of being overstaffed or understaffed, preparing succession plans and shaping the optimum future work force composition by hiring the right skill in appropriate numbers.

Need for Human Resource Planning

An organisation must plan out its human resource requirements well in advance so that it could complete effectively with its competitors in the market. A well thought-out-human resource plan provides adequate lead time for recruitment, selection and training of personnel. It becomes all the more crucial because the lead time for procuring personnel is a time consuming process and in certain cases one may not always get the requisite type of personnel needed for the jobs. Non-availability of suitable manpower may result in postponement or delays in executing new projects and expansion programmes which ultimately lead to lower efficiency and productivity further. To be specific, the following are the needs for human resource planning:

1. Shortage of Skills: These days we find shortage of skills in people. So it is necessary to plan for such skilled people much in advance than when we actually need them. Non-availability of skilled people when and where they are needed is an important factor which prompts sound Human Resource Planning.
2. Frequent Labor Turnover: Human Resource Planning is essential because of frequent labor turnover which is unavoidable by all means. Labor turnover arises because of discharges, marriages, promotion, transfer etc which causes a constant ebb and flow in the workforce in the organisation.
3. Changing needs of technology: Due to changes in technology and new techniques of production, existing employees need to be trained or new blood injected into an organisation.

4. Identify areas of surplus or shortage of personnel: Manpower planning is needed in order to identify areas with a surplus of personnel or areas in which there is a shortage of personnel. If there is a surplus, it can be re-deployed, or if there is a shortage new employees can be procured.
5. Changes in organisation design and structure: Due to changes in organisation structure and design we need to plan the required human resources right from the beginning.

Objectives of Human Resource Planning

The objective of human resource planning is to ensure the best fit between employees and jobs, while avoiding manpower shortages or surpluses. Human resource planning is a sub-system of the total organizational planning. It constitutes an integral part of corporate plan and serves the very purpose of organization in many ways. The primary purpose of human resource planning is to prepare for the future by reducing organizational uncertainty in relation to the acquisition, placement, and development of employees. Human resources planning is done to achieve the optimum use of human resources and to have the right types and correct number of employees to meet organizational goals.

The main objectives of Human Resource Planning are:

1. Achieve Goal: Human Resource Planning helps in achieving individual, Organizational & National goals. Since Human resource planning is linked with career planning, it can able to achieve individual goal while achieving organisational and national goal.
2. Estimates future organizational structure and Manpower Requirements: Human Resource Planning is related with number of Personnel required for the future, job-family, age distribution of employees, qualification & desired experience, salary range etc and thereby determines future organisation structure.
3. Human Resource Audit: Human resource planning process is comprised of estimating the future needs and determining the present supply of Manpower Resources. Manpower supply analysis is done through skills inventory. This helps in preventing over staffing as well as under-staffing.
4. Job Analysis: The process of studying and collecting information relating to operations and responsibilities of a specific job is called Job analysis. Job analysis is comprised of job description and job specification. Job description describes the duties and responsibilities of a particular job in an organized factual way. Job specification specifies minimum acceptable human qualities necessary to perform a particular job properly.

Problems with Human Resource Planning

1. Resistance by Employers: Many employers resist Human Resource Planning as they think that it increases the cost of manpower for the management. Further, employers feel that Human Resource Planning is not necessary as candidates will be available as and when required in the country due to the growing unemployment situation.
2. Resistance by Employees: Employees resist Human Resource Planning as it increases the workload on the employees and prepares programmes for securing human resources mostly from outside.
3. Inadequacies in quality of information: Reliable information about the economy, other industries, labor markets, trends in human resources etc are not easily available. This leads to problems while planning for human resources in the organisation.
4. Uncertainties: Uncertainties are quite common in human resource practices in India due to absenteeism, seasonal unemployment, labor turnover etc. Further, the uncertainties in the industrial scenario like technological changes and marketing conditions also cause imperfection in Human Resource Planning. It is the uncertainties that make Human Resource Planning less reliable.
5. Time and expense: Human Resource Planning is a time-consuming and expensive exercise. A good deal of time and cost are involved in data collection and forecasting.

Guidelines for Effective Human Resource Planning

1. Adequate information system: The main problem faced in Human Resource Planning is the lack of information. So an adequate Human resource database should be maintained/developed for better coordinated and more accurate Human Resource Planning.
2. Participation: To be successful, Human Resource Planning requires active participation and coordinated efforts on the part of operating executives. Such participation will help to improve understanding of the process and thereby, reduce resistance from the top management.
3. Adequate organisation: Human Resource Planning should be properly organised; a separate section or committee may be constituted within the human resource department to provide adequate focus and to coordinate the planning efforts at various levels.
4. Human Resource Planning should be balanced with corporate planning: Human resource plans should be balanced with the corporate plans of the enterprise. The methods and techniques used should fit the objectives, strategies and environment of the particular organisation.
5. Appropriate time horizon: The period of manpower plans should be appropriate according to the needs and circumstances of the specific enterprise. The size and structure of the enterprise as well as the changing aspirations of the people should be taken into consideration.

Factors affecting Human Resource Plans

External factor:

They are the factors which affect the Human Resource Planning externally. They include:-

1. Government policies: Policies of the government like labour policy, industrial policy, policy towards reserving certain jobs for different communities and sons-of-the-soil etc affect Human Resource Planning.
2. Level of economic development: – Level of economic development determines the level of human resource development in the country and thereby the supply of human resources in the future in the country.
3. Information Technology: Information technology brought amazing shifts in the way business operates. These shifts include Business Process Reengineering (BPR), Enterprise Resource Planning (ERP) and Supply Chain Management (SCM). These changes brought unprecedented reduction in human resource and increase in software specialists. Example: Computer-aided design (CAD) and computer-aided technology (CAT) also reduced the existing requirement of human resource.
4. Level of Technology: Technology is the application of knowledge to practical tasks which lead to new inventions and discoveries. The invention of the latest technology determines the kind of human resources required.
5. Business Environment: Business environment means the internal and external factors influencing the business. Business environmental factors influences the volume of mix of production and thereby the supply of human resources in the future in the country.
6. International factors: International factors like the demand and supply of Human resources in various countries also affects Human Resource Planning .

Internal factors:

1. Company Strategies: The organisation's policies and strategies relating to expansion, diversification etc. determines the human resource demand in terms of Quantity and Quality
2. Human Resource policies: Human Resource policies of the company regarding quality of human resources, compensation level, quality of working conditions etc. influence Human Resource Planning.
3. Job analysis: Job analysis means detailed study of the job including the skills needed for a particular job. Human Resource Planning is based on job analysis which determines the kind of employees to be procured.
4. Time Horizon: Company's planning differs according to the competitive environment i.e. companies with stable competitive environment can plan for the long run whereas firms without a stable environment can only plan for

short term. Therefore, when there are many competitors entering business/ when there is rapid change in social and economic conditions of business/ if there is constant change in demand patterns/ when there exists poor management practice, then short term planning is adopted or vice-versa for long-term planning.

5. Type and Quality of Information: Any planning process needs qualitative and accurate information about the organisational structure, capital budget, functional area objectives, level of technology being used, job analysis, recruitment sources, retirement plans, compensation levels of employees etc. Therefore Human Resource Planning is determined on the basis of the type and quality of information.
6. Company's production and operational policy: Company's policies regarding how much to produce and how much to purchase from outside in order to manufacture the final product influences the number and kind of people required.
7. Trade Unions: If the unions declare that they will not work for more than 8 hours a day, it affects the Human Resource Planning. Therefore influence of trade unions regarding the number of working hours per week, recruitment sources etc. affect Human Resource Planning.
8. Organisational Growth Cycles: At starting stage the organisation is small and the need of employees is usually smaller, but when the organisation enters the growth phase more young people need to be hired. Similarly, in the declining/recession/downturn phase Human Resource Planning is done to re-trench the employees.

Human Resource Planning Process

1. Analysis of Organisational Plans and Objectives:

Human resource planning is a part of overall plan of organization. Human resource planning process begins with the analysis of overall plan of the organization into departmental, sectional and sub-sectional plans and functional plans like sales, marketing, technological plans. This break up of overall plan provides for assessing the human resource requirement for each department and activity. Besides analyzing the organizational plans, the objectives of the organization are also analyzed.

If the objective of the organization is speedy growth and expansion, it requires more manpower in all functional activities and departments to meet the challenges of increased market share, finances, size of assets, new markets, inventory, and new products. The new growth strategy of the organization requires large number of skilled manpower. The human resource department needs to go for quick recruitment and training to meet the human resource requirement of the organization.

In case the organization facing tough times of falling demand for its products has to curtail production thereby needs to reduce manpower. The human resource department has to take some harsh decisions to retrench the existing manpower. In modern corporate world mergers and acquisitions pose fresh challenge to human resource department.

The human resource department has to face tough time because of conflicting corporate culture and working environment of the two or more firms coming together in the event of merger or acquisition. Human resource department has to formulate plans for lying off or hiring and amalgamation of conflicting cultural working environment. Sometimes the decisions regarding wage cuts have to be taken. This will displease the employees paving the way for labour unrest.

2. Analysis of Human Resource Planning Objectives:

Human resource planning is a part of corporate plan. Its objectives are to be fixed in the light of corporate objectives. The emphasis is given on future requirements than the present one. The main purpose of human resource planning is to match the present and future manpower needs of the organization.

The human resource department should specify the policy regarding acquisition of human resources. It may recruit them by way of promotion; transfer i.e. from within the organization or from external source. It also has to clarify the selection criteria and the need for training and development.

It has to decide on abolishing or continuing some old and routine jobs or replace them by meaningful new jobs to meet challenges thrown by the speedily changing business and industrial environment. These objectives should be integrated with the objectives of all the functional areas of the organization. The emphasis should also be given on to maximize the return on investment in human resources.

3. Forecasting for Human Resource Requirement:

The correct forecasting for required human resources for the organization becomes simple if design and structure of the jobs examined thoroughly keeping in view the skills, potentialities and knowledge required to perform them and make an estimate for the future requirements. It should not be taken for granted that the design and structure of the existing jobs are perfect and cannot be changed overtime. The recent development in technology and use of computers and robots in manufacturing has changed the scenario.

Now the computer aided designs (CAD) and computer aided manufacturing (CAM) has entered in ousting the traditionally used old methods. This has changed the design of jobs altogether. In modem times welding and other related jobs are done by robots.

The point is the need of capabilities, skills, knowledge, potentialities in the employees present and future must be reviewed. It will change the human resource planning. The improved techniques have not only upgraded the quality of the product but also have brought about restructuring of jobs design. The new jobs design requires more people with the knowledge of computer, engineering and other technology. There is, therefore, a growing demand for engineers and technocrats with management background by the companies.

The other factors dominating the forecast for human resources are the following:

(a) Expansion of the enterprise,

(b) Mergers and acquisitions,

(c) Retirement, death, resignation and terminations,

(d) Change in style of leadership,

(e) Improvement in productivity.

The above factors dominate the quality and quantity of the human resources. The various skills required to perform the jobs will enable the forecasting of human resource requirement for the organization. Determining the skill needs and fulfilling them is vital aspect of human resource planning. The demand for human resources is forecasted by using some statistical and work study methods and managers opinions regarding the manpower requirements for their respective departments. This is how the forecasting of demand for quality and quantity of human resources for the whole organization is made.

4. Assessment of Supply of Human Resources:

To make assessment of supply of human resources for the organization it should begin with the current human resource inventory of the organization. It is also known as auditing of human resource to be undertaken by the departments of the organization where complete information regarding skills, abilities, qualifications, capacity for hard work is available and so also the quantity and quality of human resources manning various positions, the probable retirements.

On the basis of this information they can determine the supply of manpower which is sufficient enough to meet the departmental need or in excess or in short supply. This can be quantitatively and qualitatively worked out. The sum total of supplies of all departments shall equal the organizations supply of human resources. In this way the current or present human resource inventory is accounted for.

The supply of human resources may be less because of layoffs, dismissals, voluntary retirements, retirements, deaths etc. If the supply is less than the demand for or is inadequate to meet the requirement for human resources then it can be fulfilled through external sources. The graduates from educational institutions serve the purpose.

Also the existing manpower be asked to work extra and overtime wages may be paid to them. This is purely ad hoc arrangement. After some time the organization has to hire the required number and kind of people to meet the need.

5. Matching Demand and Supply:

It is one of the objectives of human resource planning to assess the demand for and supply of human resources and match both to know shortages and surpluses on both the side in kind and in number. This will enable the human resource department to know overstaffing or understaffing. In case of shortages of human resources to meet certain jobs in the organization and are not available in the labour market then under such circumstances it is advisable to change the objectives of the organization.

In case of shortages the human resource department should be in touch with all the known sources to meet the requirement. The human resource manager may recommend the retention plan for the employees such as higher pay, improvement in work life or to grant extension to those employees are on the verge of retirement. In case of surplus human resources in some departments then the scheme for redeployment in other departments or other job may be recommended.

If the surpluses could not be absorbed in any of the departments or jobs then in consultation with the employee's union retrenchment may be undertaken giving them full benefits under the law. A promise may be given to the retrenched employees for help to get job elsewhere or whenever vacancies exist they will be preferred. Human resource planning must get a support from the organization with relevant personnel policy statement. The human resource plan becomes an action plan for the organization as regards manpower requirement.

The organization must follow the human resource philosophy as a guiding principle. Career planning must be kept in view while planning for human resources. Any individual who joins the organization has a long way to go. During his long span he aspires high and wants that his talent should get recognition by way of further promotion on high level and should be rewarded monetarily. This is especially important for those who are professionals joining vocations. Thus an organization gets professionals or experts in particular field. It is because of this certain people are becoming professional. The career planning is a part of human resource development.

Merits or Advantages of Job Analysis:

A few advantages or merits of job analysis are-

1. Direct job-related information is given:

Job analysis provides direct and detailed information about the job and the right way to perform the duties.

The insightful information imparted is useful for the supervisors and managers as learning this they can decide the duties and requirements of the job properly and according to that select the workers.

The risks and difficulties associated with the work are also understood and the expertise and knowledge required is also known through job analysis. Hence the process of selection becomes much easier after job analysis.

2. Useful for constructing the proper Job-Employee combination:

This is a vital activity in any organization as only with the suitable workers can an organization become successful.

So the worker suitable and custom-made for the job should be hired after examination of their skills, knowledge and other requirements by the manager or supervisor.

Job Analysis helps the organizations to select suitable candidates as the workers; who can perform according to the job necessities efficiently.

3. Useful for Effectual hiring methods:

The decisions of which candidate to select and whom to reject is confusing; job evaluation makes this easy as the requirements of each job is detailed properly and only the candidates who fulfill this criterion will be selected.

4. Monitoring of performance assessment and appraisal methods:

Job Analysis is useful in reviewing the performance of the workers by making the comparison of the desired result with the actual result. By depending on this results the examination and evaluation of the performance is done; whether it has been efficient or not.

Job evaluation is essential in deciding who are responsible and dedicated workers, and also award incentives and promotions to the dedicated employees to encourage them further.

It also helps in understanding the faults of individual workers and with proper analysis, the solutions are found and good workers are made responsible for the difficult tasks so that the end outcome will be effective and wanted.

5. Assist in analyzing the instruction and progress requirements:

The practice of job analysis answers numerous difficulties and queries; the person giving the instructions and training, the time of training and instructing, the matter of instruction and training, how should the training be given and is it behavioural or technical, and the process of conducting the training. All this information and decisions are taken by job analysis.

6. It is essential for determining the worthy Compensation Package for the particular job:

To take a legitimate and valid decision about the compensation packages, benefits and grants of the workers, no amount of contemplation by the managers or supervisors will do.

Only with the help of job analysis can they come to an unbiased and indisputable decision of allowances and perks related to a specific job. The allowances and reimbursement are decided to depend on the liabilities and risks of the profession.

Demerits or Disadvantages of Job Analysis

The various drawbacks of Job Analysis are-

1. Tiresome and lengthy:

The drawback which discourages most people from doing a job analysis is the lengthy procedure and unnecessary time-consumption and time-wastage during the interviews or observations.

The prolonged time required for completing a job analysis is a major drawback and becomes more of a hindrance as the employee can change the job before the manager or supervisor has completed the job analysis.

2. Involves personal liking and biases:

Though job analysis is a very efficient method of understanding the job requirements when done properly; but most often the analysis is distorted by personal likes and dislikes.

If the manager likes one worker more than the other his personal opinions will influence the job analysis and it will not be a genuine analysis.

The biases and prejudices will always be present in job analysis since it is done by human beings and they are never free from biases and prejudices completely. This favoritism and partiality causes difficulties in collecting genuine and real information.

3. Both the basis of information and supply is small:

The size and source of the data is mostly insignificant and small as the sample size is small. This makes the source of data small and only the information collected from a few workers who may even be influenced by their own personal opinions is recorded and analyzed. Then this information of job analysis is portrayed as significant and consistent.

But in reality, this is not the case as a sample of a few workers is not enough to decide the norm and become a standard.

4. Need immense amounts of hard work and dedication:

The methods for job analysis require immense dedication and hard work for the proper completion of the analysis.

It becomes all the more difficult and complex since all the different jobs has different demands and requirements in no single outline. So the same method of job analysis and the same questions and evaluation systems will not suffice for the different jobs; tailor-made questions are required for the different jobs for their proper job analysis.

The analysis and recording of information for different jobs should be done separately to get the correct results.

5. The reviewer or the job analyst may not be suitable:

Often it occurs that the analyst himself is not worthy of doing the analysis work; with an unworthy analyst, a proper job analysis is impossible to do.

He may be unaware of the goals and aims of the job on which the job evaluation is being done. If this is the case then the job analysis is nonsense and misuse of time, effort and money. It will never be any good for the organization or the workers.

So when the analyst is not properly trained he should never be given the duty of doing job analysis; he should be rigorously trained with real and authentic information to get the sense of the real world.

6. No one can analyze mental potential through Job Analysis methods:

The last drawback seen in job analysis is that the mental aptitudes like intelligence, sentiments, knowledge and wisdom, propensity, patience and stamina are never to be seen as these are intangible characteristics of each individual.

During the questioning in job analysis, the complete mental analysis can never be done as people respond differently in diverse circumstances. Hence one can never standardize the mental ability requirements in any given job.

Job analysis gathers information on the duties and responsibilities of the job; it specifies the basic requirements and qualifications for the job. The work environment is also evaluated and assessment is done about whether the work surroundings are worker-friendly or difficult to work in.

Supervision and analysis is done on the work relationship shared by workers and the relationship with customers. In job analysis, evaluation of workers is done on the basis of knowledge, expertise, and aptitudes of the workers. Through this analysis, only the minimum requirements are taken into consideration.

Advantages and Disadvantages of Job Analysis:

S.no	Advantages	Disadvantages
1	Direct job-related information is given	Tiresome and lengthy
2	Useful for constructing the proper Job-Employee combination	Involves personal liking and biases
3	Useful for Effectual hiring methods	Both the basis of information and supply is small
4	Monitoring of performance assessment and appraisal methods	Need immense amounts of hard work and dedication
5	Assist in analyzing the instruction and progress requirements	The reviewer or the job analyst may not be suitable
6	It is essential for determining the worthy Compensation Package for the particular job	No one can analyze mental potential through Job Analysis methods

Advantages and Disadvantages

Concept of Recruitment

Recruitment might be defined as the process of searching for prospective candidates for various posts lying vacant in the organisation from out of personnel supply sources, known or developed; stimulating such personnel to apply for jobs and the preparation of Recruitment Lists of interested applicants, according to data collected.

Some popular definitions of recruitment are given below:

(1) "Recruitment is the process of searching for prospective employees and stimulating them to apply for jobs in the organization." – Edwin B. Flippo

(2) "The term recruitment applies to the process of attracting potential employees to the company." – Dalton E. McFarland

Analysis of the above definitions:

(i) The term recruitment has two dimensions:

(1) Recruitment sources

(2) Recruitment lists

(ii) Recruitment sources refer to the sources from where labour supplies could be extracted. Such sources mighty be already known to the personnel management; or might be developed – through a process of researching into new and better sources of recruitment.

(iii) On the basis of data collected from recruitment sources, recruitment lists are prepared. Recruitment lists contain the names of interested applicants; who are to be considered for selection after making such persons undergo the procedure of selection; and finally selecting the 'most suitable' out of them.

Points of comment:

The following observations could be made, on the concept of recruitment:

(i) In a country, like ours, where there is substantial unemployment of various categories of persons; to get the required number of personnel by organisations, is not difficult, at all. However, to find personnel of the type suitable for organisational purposes is not so easy. As such, recruitment process aims at stimulating good quality personnel, to apply for various jobs in the organization.

(ii) Recruitment process is one of the most significant aspects of the operative personnel management. It provides the initial supply of manpower. If, people obtained from recruitment sources are initially defective or sub-standard; no amount of subsequent training or development howsoever excellent can turn them into good personnel.

If, on the other hand, initially the recruited personnel are of superior quality; subsequent training or development can mould them into outstanding personalities. Hence, the significance of proper recruitment.

Sources of Recruitment – Internal and External:

We can identify two basic sources of recruitment,

1. Internal sources
2. External sources

(i) Internal sources:

Internal sources of recruitment are those through which, the manpower supplies are obtained, out of the personnel, already working in the organisation or out of the ex-employees of the organization.

(ii) External sources:

External sources of recruitment refer to those sources which ensure supply of manpower, from out of the environmental labour market traced via different means like advertising, employment exchangers, labour contractors, and other means.

Internal Sources – Types, Merits and Limitations:

Internal sources of recruitment are:

(i) Promotions/demotions of existing employees

(ii) Transfers of existing employees

(iii) Appointment of ex-employees

Following is a brief account of the above internal sources of recruitment.

(i) Promotions/demotions of existing employees:

Promotion means an upward placement of an existing employee on a higher level job involving more responsibility coupled with higher status, and carrying more remuneration and perks. Demotion is the reverse of promotion. It means a downward placement of an existing employee on a lower level job involving less responsibility coupled with lower status, and carrying less remuneration and perks.

Point of comment:

Promotions/demotions are not really sources of recruitment; because, there is need to fill up afresh those positions with suitable persons which have been vacated by the promoted or demoted personnel. These are a source of recruitment, only in cases, when the positions vacated by promoted or demoted personnel are regarded as absolutely unnecessary by management – requiring no replacements.

However, as a matter of policy, the management might promote deserving personnel, on the basis of seniority or merit. In that sense, promotion becomes a source of internal recruitment; while requiring, at the same time, some external / internal source of recruitment to fill up the position vacated by the promoted person.

Similarly, demotions might be resorted to, effect remedial adjustment, in the original placement of employees. Here also, a new problem of replacement arises – to fill up the positions, vacated by the demoted personnel.

(ii) Transfers of existing employees:

Transfer means placement of existing employees, on jobs, almost similar to those, occupied by transferees, prior to transfer, carrying similar types of responsibilities, work, and remuneration etc. at some new place within the same enterprise, or some other branch of the enterprise.

Transfers may be effected by management to remedy the situations created by misplacements, or as a matter of policy of not allowing a person to occupy a particular position permanently for reasons of avoiding misappropriation of money and property or other unhealthy tactics likely to develop through secret collusions among 'permanently fixed' employees.

The latter type of transfer philosophy is particularly observed by managements of banking institutions.

Point of comment:

Transfers of employees, affected by whatever causes, are also not a real source of internal recruitment; as there is a need to fill up afresh the positions, vacated by the transferees. This requires external recruitment. Transfers may be a source of recruitment, only in cases, when the positions vacated by the transferees are regarded as absolutely unnecessary by the management – requiring no replacements.

(iii) Appointment of ex-employees:

Sometimes ex-employees of an organization might be recalled; and assigned to suitable posts, in the organization. We can visualize two types of situations, under this source of recruitment.

(a) Recalling of ex-military personnel, in case of military organizations, specially in emergency situations, e.g. the outbreak of war.

(b) Recalling laid-off or retrenched employees, by any organization, provided such personnel are willing to rejoin the organization and are otherwise available i.e. they have not got alternative employment, elsewhere, outside the organization.

Point of comment:

Appointment of ex-employees, is a real source of internal recruitment; provided ex-personnel are willing to rejoin the organization and are also available.

Merits of Internal Sources of Recruitment:

Some of the important merits of internal sources of recruitment are:

(i) Easy Availability:

From the internal sources of recruitment, personnel are easily available, especially in cases of promotions and transfers. In case of ex-employees, their fresh recruitment is, of course, possible; if these are available (i.e. not employed elsewhere) and are willing to re-join the organization. However, in military organizations, ex-military personnel might be forcibly recruited afresh – as per the military norms and rules.

(ii) No Recruitment Costs:

Internal sources of recruitment do not entail any substantial recruitment costs; as recruitment lists can be prepared without much time, efforts and costs, by management – on the basis of past personnel records.

(iii) Selection Procedure Formalities not Required:

In all business enterprises, there is a specified selection procedure to be undergone by aspiring candidates for being finally selected. These selection procedure formalities are naturally rendered unnecessary, in case of internal sources of recruitment; as the existing personnel or the ex-employees of the organisation had already cleared through the 'selection hurdles' on prior occasions.

(iv) No Need for Orientation:

Existing employees or ex-employees of the organization do not require any induction or orientation; as these are already introduced to the organization; and can be immediately placed on suitable positions, in the organization.

(v) High Morale and Reduced Labour Turnover:

Internal sources of recruitment lead to high employee morale. This advantage is specifically applicable in case of promotions; when promotions are to be made, on the basis of seniority – as per the promotion policy of the organization. An added advantage here is that of reduced labour turnover.

When employees know that they are to be promoted on the basis of seniority; they feel more inclined to stay, in the organization waiting for their turn to claim promotion and thus making for a stable labour force.

(vi) Correcting Faults in Placements:

Through effecting demotions and transfers of existing employees, internal sources of recruitment, provide an opportunity to management to correct defects in the original placement of employees.

(vii) To Break Monotony of Old Jobs:

Internal sources of recruitment help employees to break the monotony of old jobs. By effecting suitable transfers, this advantage can be availed of.

(viii) To Enrich Experience of Existing Employees:

Internal sources of recruitment enable management to enrich the experience of existing employees by effecting 'pleasant transfers' and resorting to promotions of employees on new and challenging jobs.

Limitations of Internal Sources of Recruitment:

Some of the major limitations of internal sources of recruitment are as follows:

(i) Fresh Talent from Outside, not Availed of:

Internal sources of recruitment limit the talent only to the 'limited talents' of the existing employees. Fresh talent from outside sources is ruled out, under this method of recruitment. This disadvantage may specially tell upon the prosperity of the enterprise; when all promotions are exclusively guided by the 'seniority-criterion.'

(ii) Favoritism and Nepotism:

Internal sources of recruitment invite or encourage favoritism and nepotism, on the part of management, while resorting to promotions of employees, on the basis of merit; as there are no 'full- proof' techniques of measuring the merit of employees.

This disadvantage of favoritism and nepotism emanating from internal sources of recruitment might lead to spoiling human relations in the organization. At the same time, meritorious employees might become negligent in their work in future when denied 'deserved promotions.'

Merits and limitations of internal source of recruitment - at a glance

Merits :

1. Easy availability
2. No recruitment costs
3. Selection procedure formalities, not required
4. No need for orientation
5. High morale and reduced labour turnover
6. Correcting faults in placements
7. To break monotony of old jobs
8. To enrich experience of existing employees.

Limitations

1. Fresh talent form outside not availed of
2. Favouritism and nepotism
3. Limited source
4. Unsuitable for newer type of jobs
5. Personnel of advanced age

Merits and Limitations of Internal Source of Recruitment

(iii) Limited Source:

Internal sources are only a limited source of recruitment. When a large number of personnel are required for promotions or placement on additional jobs created by the expansion of the enterprise; internal sources have to be supplemented by external recruitment sources.

(iv) Unsuitable for Newer Types of Jobs:

When certain newer types of jobs are created in an organization, because of a restructuring of manner of functioning of the organization; internal sources of recruitment might fail to serve the purpose of management. This is so because, existing employees are accustomed to the old style of organizational functioning; and might not be confident and competent to handle the newer types of jobs effectively.

(v) Personnel of Advanced Age:

Internal sources of recruitment can make available to organization, personnel of advanced age; as they have already served the organization, for, at least, some time, in the past. The danger with 'advanced age personnel' is that, most of them would be soon attaining the age of retirement necessitating fresh replacements from external recruitment sources after some time.

External Sources

Important sources of external recruitment might be mentioned as follows:

(i) Advertisements

(ii) Employment exchanges

(iii) Campus recruitment i.e. educational and technical institutions

(iv) Jobbers or contractors / personnel consultants

(v) Recruitment at the factory gate or gate hiring.

(vi) Waiting lists of unsolicited applicants.

(vii) Recommendations of existing employees.

(viii) Labour union recommendations

(ix)Field trips

(x)Recruitment through leasing / deputation

Following is a brief account of the above mentioned sources of external recruitment:

(i) Advertisements:

In the present-day-times, a popular method of external recruitment is, advertising the vacancies.

Vacancies might be advertised through the following media:

(a) Press:

Including leading newspapers, local dailies, trade magazines and journals, household magazines etc.

(b) Audio or Audio-visual Media:

Including radio, TV, cinema. The task of advertising vacancies might be undertaken by the organization itself; or entrusted to some professional advertising agency. However, in any case, the advertisements must be properly designed or planned containing a brief but relevant account of job description, job specification and terms and conditions of the contract of service- emphasizing, in particular, on the remuneration aspect.

(ii) Employment Exchanges:

Recruitment through employment exchange is, perhaps, the most popular medium of external recruitment now-a-days. Employment exchanges are institutions which register the names of unemployed persons, seeking various types of jobs; and keep in touch with employers, who require the types of personnel, registered with them.

Employment exchanges might be, Public Employment Exchanges i.e. established by the State, or Private Employment Exchanges i.e. established by private organisations.

In the former case, i.e. public employment exchanges, there are usually, separate exchanges for unskilled, semi-skilled and technical types of personnel. Private employment exchanges more often, specialize, in the registration or personnel aspiring for management cadre jobs or technical type of jobs.

Point of comment:

Recruitment through the forum of public employment exchanges is, of course, compulsory for public enterprises and for some categories of private employers.

(iii) Campus Recruitment i.e. Educational and Technical Institutions:

This source of recruitment relates to getting personnel from schools, colleges, universities and technical institutes. Representatives or agents of employers visit these educational institutions and make a first-hand recruitment of willing personnel whom they have a chance to contact, for certain jobs, existing with their employers.

Alternatively, the employers might contact the Heads of educational institutions; requesting them to suggest and send the names of promising students of their institutions, for recruitment to various posts, lying vacant, in their organizations. Campus recruitment is often resorted to by employers; when they want personnel of high academic qualifications, specially for managerial jobs or technical type of jobs.

(iv) Jobbers or Contractors/Personnel Consultants:

Jobbers or contractors are professional persons who keep in touch with potential laborers waiting for work, existing in cities and villages; but specially villages.

At the same time, these jobbers / contractors, maintain contacts with employers, who would require personnel available with them; and supply the requisite number and quality of personnel to the latter charging commission, for their services. However, this source of recruitment through jobbers or contractors is suitable for unskilled type of personnel.

A counterpart of jobbers or contractors is personnel consultants; who provide similar type of services, for making available the skilled personnel for managerial jobs or technical jobs, to various organizations. They keep in touch with both the qualified personnel, (in the recruitment of which they specialize) and the employers, interested in those types of personnel.

However, unlike jobbers or contractors, personnel consultants, usually, charge quite high, for their services to employers.

(v) Recruitment at the Factory Gate or Gate Hiring:

It is a common practice, still today, in India, for unskilled labourers to throng factory gates; aspiring for getting jobs-temporary or permanent. Management can recruit personnel, out of this source, in the number required by it – on the basis of preliminary interview or interrogation.

(vi) Waiting Lists of Unsolicited Applicants:

It is usual practice for unemployed people to be driven from pillar to post (i.e. from one employer to other) in search of jobs, suitable for their abilities and qualifications. This source of recruitment is known as unsolicited applicants or causal callers. Unsolicited applicants may or may not get jobs of their suitability – depending on the availability of vacancies, with the employer.

Managements of various organizations, however, have the practice of maintaining waiting lists of such unsolicited applicants; and might make a call on them at times, when a need for such personnel is felt by the organization. It is, of course, a casual source of recruitment.

(vii) Recommendations of Existing Employees:

Some organizations make a certain percentage of the recruitment of personnel – on the basis of the recommendations of the existing employees i.e. existing employees of the organization might be asked to recommend the names of their friends, relatives or acquaintances – for recruitment to various posts lying vacant in the organization.

Existing employees, in fact, act as intermediaries or middlemen for recruitment purposes; who know well both their friends, relatives and acquaintances, and the organization, they are employed in; and can make suitable recommendations to management about likely recruits.

This source of recruitment adds to loyalty and dedication of existing employees; who not only plan to stay for longer periods in the organization, for enabling themselves to recommend to management the names of those known to them; but also, serve a useful purpose of management by making available reliable persons.

Point of comment:

This source of recruitment is adopted, as a matter of management policy, in many organizations, particularly banking institutions; where men of trust and confidence are required in view of the nature of business.

(viii) Labour Union Recommendations:

Under this source of recruitment, the management of a business enterprise might invite recommendations from the leaders of labour unions, to suggest the names of suitable personnel, for recruitment to certain jobs, lying vacant in the organization.

This method of recruitment serves a double purpose. For one thing, the management can get good personnel of trust and confidence, on the genuine recommendations of labour union leaders; and for another, this system of recruitment helps to develop good "labour management relations", by pleasing union leaders.

Sometimes, there might be an agreement between management and labour union leaders, whereby, at least some agreed percentage of personnel must be recruited on the recommendations of the labour union.

(ix) Field Trips:

Under this system of recruitment, organizations send their labour experts to different places – towns and cities for making a search for good technical and managerial personnel. However, recruitment through this source is only a matter of chance; in that the agents of organization may or may not come across the requisite type of qualified personnel.

(x) Recruitment through Leasing /Deputation:

Recruitment through leasing / deputation refers to hiring personnel – specially managerial and technical – from other established enterprises. This system of recruitment is usually adopted by public enterprises, in the initial stages of their development; when outstanding managerial and technical personnel are hired on lease basis or deputation, from eminent private enterprises.

Depending on the terms of agreement between the two organizations; such personnel hired on lease / deputation basis might stay permanently with the new organization or revert to their old organization.

Manpower Planning

Manpower Planning which is also called as Human Resource Planning consists of putting right number of people, right kind of people at the right place, right time, doing the right things for which they are suited for the achievement of goals of the organization. Human Resource Planning has got an important place in the arena of industrialization. Human Resource Planning has to be a systems approach and is carried out in a set procedure. The procedure is as follows:

- Analysing the current manpower inventory
- Making future manpower forecasts
- Developing employment programmes
- Design training programmes

Steps in Manpower Planning

1) **Analysing the current manpower inventory**- Before a manager makes forecast of future manpower, the current manpower status has to be analysed. For this the following things have to be noted-

- Type of organization
- Number of departments
- Number and quantity of such departments
- Employees in these work units

Once these factors are registered by a manager, he goes for the future forecasting.

2) **Making future manpower forecasts**- Once the factors affecting the future manpower forecasts are known, planning can be done for the future manpower requirements in several work units.

The Manpower forecasting techniques commonly employed by the organizations are as follows:

- Expert Forecasts: This includes informal decisions, formal expert surveys and Delphi technique.

- Trend Analysis: Manpower needs can be projected through extrapolation (projecting past trends), indexation (using base year as basis), and statistical analysis (central tendency measure).
- Work Load Analysis: It is dependent upon the nature of work load in a department, in a branch or in a division.
- Work Force Analysis: Whenever production and time period has to be analysed, due allowances have to be made for getting net manpower requirements.
- Other methods: Several Mathematical models, with the aid of computers are used to forecast manpower needs, like budget and planning analysis, regression, new venture analysis.

3) **Developing employment programmes**- Once the current inventory is compared with future forecasts, the employment programmes can be framed and developed accordingly, which will include recruitment, selection procedures and placement plans.

4) **Design training programmes**- These will be based upon extent of diversification, expansion plans, development programmes,etc. Training programmes depend upon the extent of improvement in technology and advancement to take place. It is also done to improve upon the skills, capabilities, knowledge of the workers.

Steps in Manpower Planning Process:

The steps in manpower planning are discussed below:

1. **Forecasting Staffing Needs:**

The first step in the manpower planning process involves forecasting staffing needs and determining the actions needed to fulfill those needs. The most important step in forecasting staffing needs is a review of the organisation's objectives and strategies.

This includes reviews at both the corporate enterprise level and the business unit level. If the organization is pursuing growth objectives then there may be a need to expand the size of the firm's human resources.

2. **Forecasting Internal Supply**:

Once staffing needs have been forecast, managers are in a position to forecast the internal supply of human resources. A forecast of internal supply is derived from examining the kinds of human resources internal to the organization, the demo-graphics of those resources (especially years until retirement), and the stability of the people presently employed.

This process may include a job analysis, which is a systematic study of what is done, when, where, how, why, and by whom in current and predicted jobs. The job analysis can be used to write job descriptions and job specifications.

A job description is a written statement of job duties and responsibilities. A job description frequently includes working conditions, and the tools, materials, and equipment used to perform the job. A job specification is a list of the skills, abilities, education, experience, and other qualifications needed for the job.

The job analysis may include a human resource audit. A human resource audit is a listing of the strengths and weaknesses of current personnel. For example, such an audit may uncover weakness in the information technology skills of current employees at a time when the organization is entering a computer system intense business.

3. **Forecasting External Supply:**

Once managers have forecast internal supply, they are in a position to forecast external supply. As with forecasting internal supply, this includes a review of skills, abilities, education, experience, and other qualifications needed for the job. Especially if the organization has always hired locally, this forecast may have implications for training to fill gaps.

4. **Correcting Shortage or Surplus:**

From the forecasts and the comparisons of supplies and needs, the organization is in a position to correct the imbalances. If there is a surplus in the organization, management needs to decide the value of the human resources to the enterprise and if it will carry a surplus until normal turnover and retirements correct the situation.

If there is a huge imbalance and if management cannot tolerate the costs of carrying the surplus personnel then it might resort to involuntary pay cuts, part-time work, early retirements, and terminations. Alternatively, if there is a shortage of human resources in certain areas, cross training and hiring seem to be the only alternatives.

Thus the four stages of the manpower planning process are:

1. An evaluation or appreciation of existing manpower resources.
2. An estimation of the proportion of currently employed manpower resources which are likely to be within the firm by the forecast date.
3. An assessment or forecast of labour requirements if the organisation's over¬all objectives are to be achieved by the forecast date.
4. Adoption of required measures to ensure that the necessary resources are available as and when required, that is, the manpower plan.

While stages 1 and 2 are linked with the supply aspect of manpower, stage 3 represents the demand aspect of manpower.

Analysing training and development needs is the final part of a manpower planning effort.

Here the questions to be answered are:

(a) How many people need training and development?

(b) Who are the specific individuals? and

(c) What kind of training is needed?

These are the problems which a personnel manager has to face and solve.

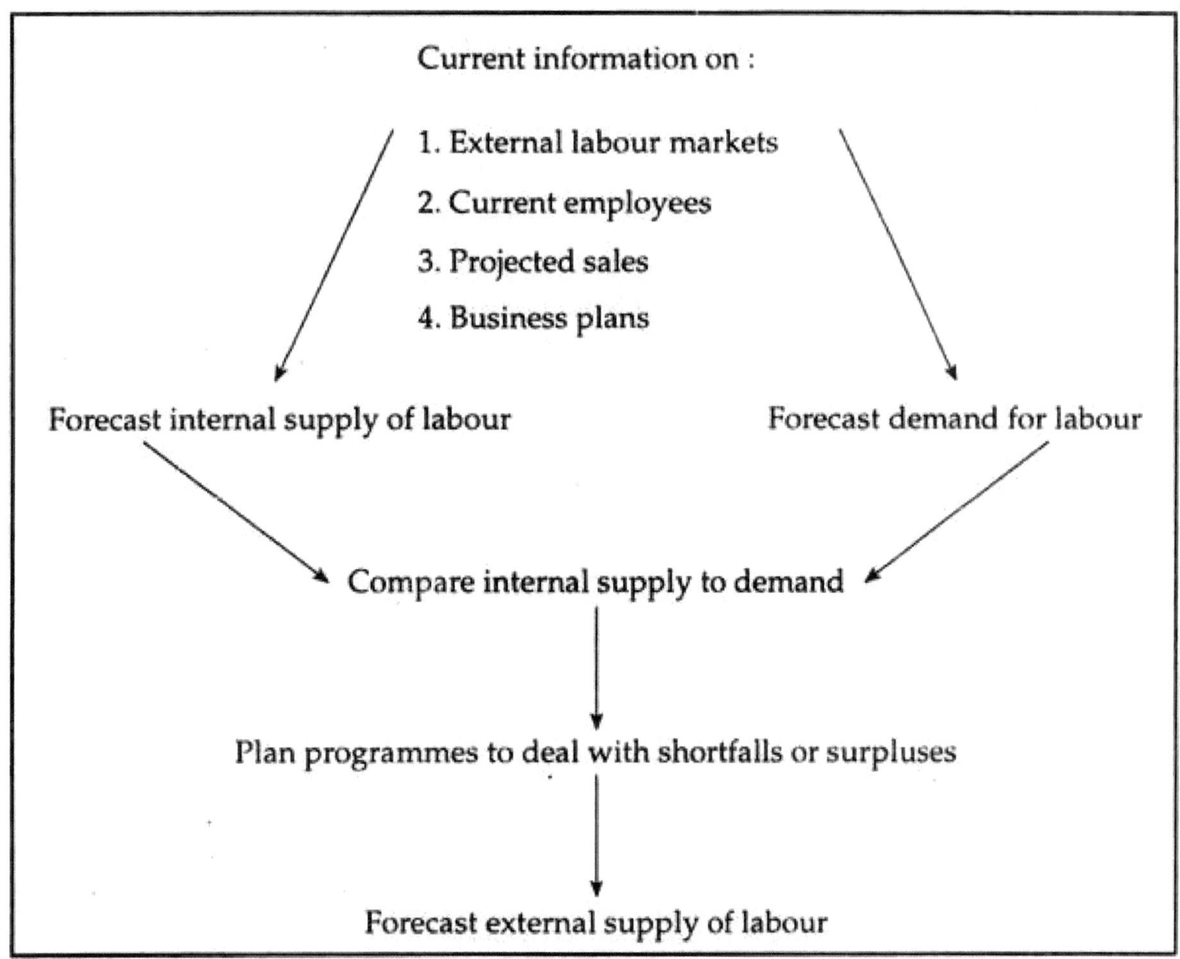

A Schematic Representation of Manpower Planning

Manpower planning consists of forecasting the organization's future needs for employees, and then planning programmes to meet unfilled needs so that the organization will have the right number and kind of employees when they are needed.

Effective manpower planning starts with a forecast. The human resource forecast estimates the number and types of employees the organisation will need over the next one to two years. The forecast also predicts the supply of employees to fill these needs. In predicting supply, the human resource manager considers internal sources, or employees who could be promoted or shifted into the vacant positions, as well as external sources: people currently in school, working for another company, or actively seeking employment.

Techniques of Manpower Planning:

We have already noted that manpower planning involves forecasting manpower needs, assessing manpower supply and reconciling supply and demand through various personnel-related programmes. The manpower planning process is affected by the organization's strategic management decisions and environmental uncertainties.

These two factors, in turn, determine the length of the planning horizons, the type and quality of information available to manpower planners and the nature of jobs to be filled. Manpower demand forecasts and assessments of supply must be continuously monitored so that adjustments can be made in the programmes de¬signed to reconcile the supply and demand of manpower resources.

1. Forecasting Manpower Needs (Demand):

Manpower demand refers the total human resource needs of an organization for a given time period. The precise nature of an organization's demand for manpower depends on various factors. Once the factors affecting the demand for manpower are identified, methods for forecasting can be designed and implemented.

External factors include competition (foreign and domestic), the economic climate (such as the stock market crash of 1992), laws and regulations and changes in technology. Internal factors include budget constraints, production levels, new products and services and organizational structure.

2. Short-term Forecasting:

Short-range forecasts usually grow out of normal budgetary processes. Manpower budgets and projections are generally based on estimates of work-loads (production schedules, passenger loads, expansions or contractions in operations).

Conversion ratios that translate workload data into manpower demand estimates may be used for a short-range demand forecast. For example, as sales increase by a certain percentage, a manufacturing concern may determine by how much the number of employees in certain departments or divisions must also increase.

The use of conversion ratios provides only a rough approximation of the number of employees required and may indicate very little about the types of manpower needed. It is important for an organization to carefully define not only the number of workers needed by the entire organization, but also the type required at various levels, departments and locations. Job analysis information is hopeful in this respect, because it defines the educational, experience and skill requirements of future employees.

3. Long-term Forecasting:

This is done with mathematical and statistical models. Unlike forecasting short-term needs, which generally involves necessary adjustments, to assure that specific vacan-cies are filled, long-term forecasts are more general in nature.

Mathematical models used in manpower forecasting are based on selected key variables that affect the organization's overall manpower needs. Some models contain both internal and external variables. For example, a model incorporating the following factors might be used to forecast overall employment in an organization:

$$\text{En} = \frac{(\text{Lagg} + \text{G})\,\frac{1}{X}}{Y}$$

where En is the estimated level of manpower demand in n planning periods (e.g., years); Lagg is the overall aggregate level of current business activity in rupees and, G is the total growth in business activity anticipated through period n in today's rupees.

X is the average productivity improvement anticipated from today through planning period n (e.g., if X = 1.80 it means an average productivity improvement of 8%).

Y is an conversion figure relating today's overall activity to manpower required (total level of today's business activity) divided by the current number of personnel). It reflects the level of business activity per person.

The major purpose of this model is to predict En, the level of manpower necessary in n periods. Before putting the number into the model, estimates of G, X and Y must be made." Such estimates may be based on the previous experiences of management, as well as on future strategic choices to which the organization's decision-makers are committed.

The application of a personnel (employment) forecasting model depends heavily on obtaining accurate estimates of total growth (G), average productivity improvement (X) and conversion ratios (Y) (e.g., one employee per Rs 50,000 in sales).

Suppose we wish to estimate the number of salespersons necessary in 2000. We may use the relationship between sales and the number of salespersons we have today as a starting point. Let's assume that we currently have Rs 1,000,000 in sales today (Lagg).

We also assume that by 2000 our sales will increase by Rs 500,000 in today's rupees (G, rupees adjusted for inflation), that there will be no increase in productivity (X = 1.0), and each of today's employees can support Rs 50,000 worth of sales (X). If we substitute these values into the formula we obtain

$$\text{En} = \frac{(\text{Lagg} + \text{G})\,\frac{1}{X}}{Y}$$

$$E_{1999} = \frac{(\text{Rs } 1{,}000{,}000 + \text{ Rs } 500{,}000)\,\frac{1}{1.0}}{50{,}000}$$

$$E_{1999} = \frac{(\text{Rs } 1{,}500{,}000)^{8}}{50{,}000} = \text{ 30 salespersons}$$

4. Linear Regression:

Another quantitative approach, viz., linear regression analysis, may also be used to estimate the manpower necessary at a future point in time, based upon such factors as sales, output or services rendered. For example, if a college is expanding, it is likely that more teachers will be needed.

If there has been a satisfactory relationship in the past between the size^>f the faculty and the number of students enrolled, linear regression may be a useful method for estimating the number of teachers needed for expansion.

The following straight line equation may be used:

Y = α + βX

where Y = the number of faculty and X = the number of students enrolled.

If we wish to estimate the number of faculty needed in 2000, we may substitute the expected 1998 enrollment into the equation.

Another approach to determining the number of faculty members required in 2000 involves using a graph to locate the estimated number of students in 2000 on the X-axis, plot a vertical line up to the regression line and then plot a horizontal line over to the Y-axis, reading the necessary number of faculty from the Y-axis (see dotted line in Fig. below).

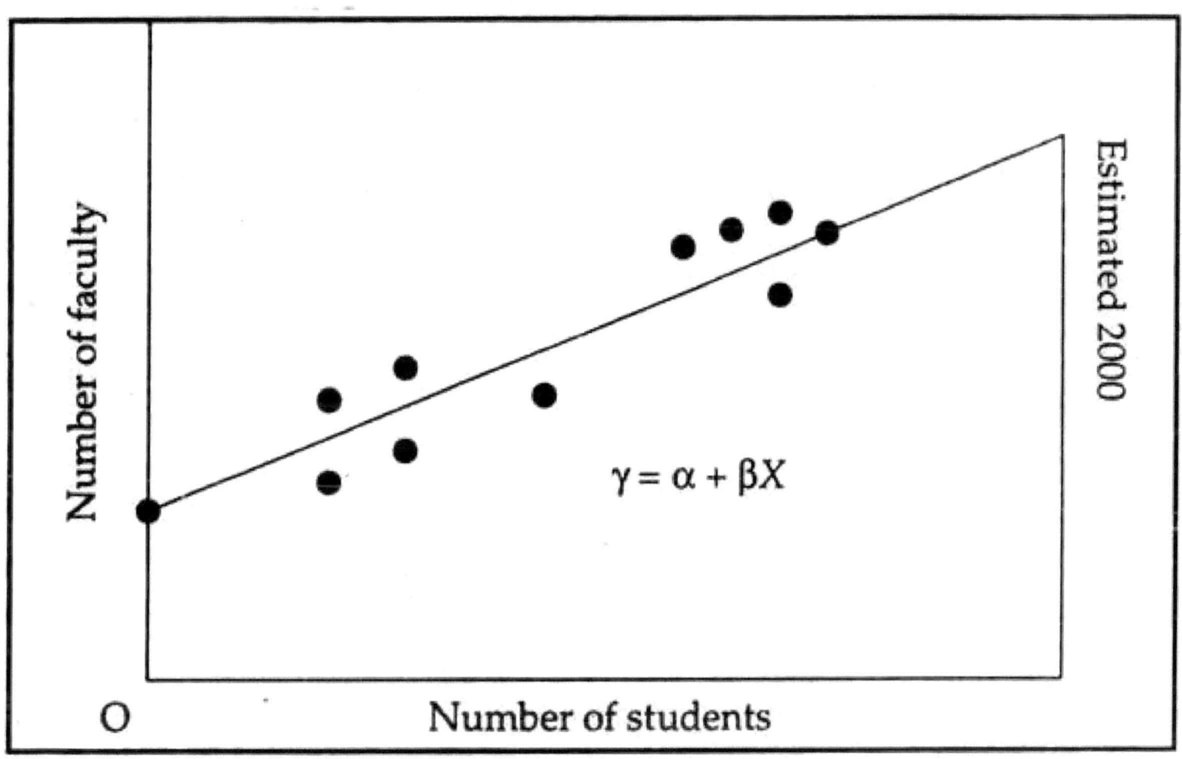

Linear Regression Line

If the graph is precise, one will read the same value for the necessary faculty as one would get using the above equation. The entire process depends upon the accuracy of one's estimation of student enrollment in 2000. If the estimate of likely student enrollment in 2000 is inaccurate, then the prediction based upon it is less likely to be accurate.

The quantitative approaches presented here (conversion ratios, aggregate plan¬ning model and linear regression) represent only-three methods from among many that are available. When using linear regression it is very important that the equation accurately summarizes the past relationship between the two variables.

Some organizations use group estimation to obtain long-term forecasts. The complexity of organizations and the environments in which they must exist makes forecasting input from numerous individuals each of whom is an expert in his or her specialization especially useful.

Although the group estimation models used may vary somewhat, most of them involve the following steps:

1. Selecting a variety of specialists or experts throughout the organization who possess knowledge or expertise relevant to the manpower forecast.

2. Identifying key forecasting concerns, variables, problems and developments through scrutiny of the organization's strategic position.

3. Developing a list of specific manpower forecasting questions or issues that must be addressed by the group.

4. Designing a system such as a questionnaire that will enable each specialist or expert to have input into the forecasting process.

5. Once input is received and placed in an organized form, the group leader attempts to gain a general agreement on the manpower.

5. Forecasting Manpower Supply:

Manpower planners must consider both the external supply (employees available for hire in the organization's geographic workforce) and the internal supply (the organization's current employees) of human resources.

It is important for personnel planners to anticipate and pinpoint changes in personnel supply. Various methods are available for doing this. A relatively straightforward method is presented in Fig. above.

Although manpower planning is concerned with having an adequate number of employees to fill positions within the organization, it is equally concerned with providing the right type of person for the job. A major function of manpower planning is to examine the skills and capabilities of current employees in light of the organisation's short- and long-term needs.

Inventories form the basis of promotion, transfer, layoff and training and development decisions. In essence, skills inventories provide an information base for monitoring an employee's potential contribution to the organisation, making informed personnel-related decisions, and, in general, assessing the organisation's manpower supply.

Manpower information systems provide a means of collecting, summarising and analysing data to find out the manpower requirement. Information requirements associated with the personnel function are numerous. For example, assessing per-sonnel supply involves keeping track of employees throughout the organisation.

6. Balancing Manpower Supply and Demand:

Once an organization's manpower needs (demand) are determined and the current supply of employees is assessed, then manpower supply and demand must be balanced in order that vacancies can be filled by the right employee at the proper time. Balancing supply and demand is largely a matter of planning, timing and use of various personnel-related programmes to achieve the desired results.

Uses:

The many activities included in the personnel management function start with manpower planning which refers to the process of forecasting personnel needs and developing the necessary strategies for meeting those needs.

This information helps managers in several ways:

1. Managers can anticipate personnel shortages or vacancies and act to create or fill jobs before problems arise.

2. Managers can anticipate the types of training and development the personnel will need.

3. Managers can identify the particular skills and abilities of the present employ¬ees to help develop effective career paths for them.

4. Managers can evaluate the effect of human resource decisions and make any necessary changes.

5. Inventories of employee skills are often maintained in computerized files. They include information about each employee's educational and training background, experience, and special skills (e.g., foreign language proficiency). With the use of skill inventories, personnel managers can readily identify what skills are available in the internal labour market and what skills must be imported from the external labour market.

6. Staffing changes -due to retirements, sick leaves and occasional personal emer-gencies must also be anticipated. This involves little more than keeping track of the ages of employees and being careful to take account of absent employees and positions vacated by promotions and transfers.

However, when staffing changes are due to changes in programmes or departments, manpower planning becomes more complicated. Budgetary considerations come into play. Employees associated with obsolete programmes generally will not be kept on unless they can be retrained or their skills utilised elsewhere.

More and more organizations are instituting manpower planning systems. Short- term planning (one to two years) to guide immediate recruiting needs is most common, but mid- and long-range planning (up to ten years) can also be helpful, especially for managerial jobs. When we foresee a need for many more middle managers in seven years' time, we had better begin right away to locate and develop individuals with management potential.

Recruitment and Selection Policy

1. SUITABILITY

Writing an accurate position description is an important part of the recruitment process. It describes the primary tasks involved as well as the core competencies required to perform the role.

A good recruitment and selection policy would require those writing job descriptions to give precedence to the competencies that would make the most positive contribution to the organization's business requirements (i.e. flexibility, initiative, leadership etc).

2. CONSISTENCY

A good recruitment and selection policy will also require that hiring managers use pre-determined criteria at all stages of the recruitment process, thereby reducing the risk of bias or discrimination.

In the screening stage, the key selection criteria should have been determined before the job was advertised and clearly displayed in the advertisement and job description.

Each candidate would then be evaluated according to those criteria only. When interviewing candidates, the same interviewers should be present at each interview and a set of pre-determined questions asked of each candidate, allowing them equal time to respond.

Reference checks should be conducted before any appointment is made and should be carried out in a consistent manner (i.e. asking similar questions of each candidate's referees and former employers).

It should be noted that treating everyone consistently does not always imply fairness. If a candidate is at a disadvantage for any reason (i.e. has a disability), you may need to take their individual circumstances into account, so they are given an equal opportunity to present their case.

3. LEGALITY

Privacy and equal opportunity legislation require that the recruitment process is conducted in a fair and transparent manner and a good recruitment and selection policy will always make this very clear to recruiters.

During no stage of the recruitment process (from advertisement to interview) can there be any discriminatory behavior, based on a person's age, sex, marital status, religion, nationality, sexual orientation or disability.

A candidate may have recourse to legal action if they feel they have been discriminated against, so impartiality is not only the right thing to do, it's also good risk management practice.

Discrimination may be quite unintentional.

For example, using terms in a job advertisement such as 'young and energetic' or 'new graduate' may seem harmless enough, but should be avoided as they are implying that you must be young to apply for the job.

Privacy laws also require that a candidate's application is treated confidentially. Penalties apply if breaches occur, so here as well, a good recruitment and selection policy helps to protect the organization's best interests.

An example of a privacy breach would be a recruiter discussing the details of a confidential job application with their family or friends. A recruitment and selection policy that reminds staff about the implications of possible lapses such as these can go a long way towards ensuring they never happen.

4. CREDIBILITY

Not all job advertisements are genuine.

Some are placed by organizations wishing to build up a 'talent pool' or to simply to test the waters and see what's out there.

If an organization calls for certain application procedures to be followed, candidates can feel confident the position they are applying for actually exists and that their efforts will not be in vain.

Candidates can also see you are a reputable employer by the good practices you follow and are more likely to want to become an employee of your organization.

5. TRANSPARENCY

By requiring transparent procedures at every step, the recruitment and selection policy ensures that all stakeholders in the recruitment process (HR, department head, line manager etc) are able to follow the process and be confident of the outcome.

Candidates should be kept informed of the status of their application and notified if unsuccessful. Reasons for decisions made during the recruitment process should be documented and a transparent appeals process put in place if a candidate is unhappy with the outcome.

Principle of Recruitment Policy

Below mention Principles must followed while recruiting employees:

- As per company Policy, it believes in the open competition ways for recruitment.
- The company makes sure that the right and meritorious candidate is hired through the recruitment process and it also ensures that most suitable candidate is identified.
- The company makes sure that the recruitment and selection of candidate happen in a professional way and by following the rules and regulations under employment legislation.
- The company also ensures that all its employees involved in the recruitment and selection process are well trained. The company provides training to all its employees to make them satisfied that they are well trained to carry on recruitment and they comply with the regulations under employment policy.
- The recruitment must be carried out in a manner that enhances the image of the company outside.
- The company also put in best efforts to carry out the process in a transparent and effective manner wherein all candidates are treated equally and fairly so that recruitment experience is a positive one in the company.
- The company believes in inculcating new and innovative practice in its recruitment process and will promote best practice.
- The company also tries its best to make sure that this process is carried out in a very cost-effective manner.
- Any employee in recruitment team who has a close relationship with any of the candidate applying for any position in the company must make sure that it is declared by the employee in the beginning of recruitment process and he/she will not be involved in any decision-making process.
- All the information provided by the candidate must be treated with confidentiality and must not be shared with any third agency.

Internal and External Factors which affects the Recruitment Process in human resource management

Internal Factors

The internal factors likewise term as endogenous elements are the components inside the association that impact selecting in the organization

The internal forces i.e. the factors which can be controlled by the organization are:

1. Recruitment Policy

The recruitment policy of the organization i.e. recruiting from internal sources and external also affect the recruitment process. The recruitment policy of an organization determines the destinations or enlistment and gives a structure to usage of recruitment program.

Factors Affecting Recruitment Policy

- Need of the organization.
- Organizational objectives
- Preferred sources of recruitment.
- Government policies on reservations.
- Personnel policies of the organization and its competitors.
- Recruitment costs and financial implications.

2. Human Resource Planning

Effective human resource process and procedure helps in fixing the loops present in the existing manpower of the organization. This also helps in filter the number of employees to be recruited and what kind qualification and skills they must possess.

3. Size of the Organization

The size of the organization affects the recruitment process. If the organization is planning to increase its operations and expand its business, it will think of hiring more personnel, which will handle its operations.

4. Cost involved in recruitment

Recruitment process also count the cost to the employer, thats why organizations try to employ/outsource the source of recruitment, which will be cost effective to the organization for each candidate.

5. Growth and Expansion

Organization will utilize or consider utilizing more work force in the event that it is growing its operations.

External Factors

The external forces are the forces which cannot be controlled by the organization. The major external forces are:

1. Supply and Demand

The availability of manpower both within and outside the organization is an essential factor in the recruitment process.

2. Labour Market

Employment conditions where the organization is located will effected by the recruiting efforts of the organization.

3. Goodwill / Image of the organization

Image of the firm is another factor having its effect on the Different government controls forbidding separation in contracting and work have coordinate effect on enlistment practices. As taken Example, Govt. of India has the convention of reservation in work for booked standings/planned clans, physically Disabled and so on. Additionally, exchange associations have the significant part in enrollment. This limits management freedom to select those individuals who can be the best performers. This can work as a potential constraint for recruitment. A company with positive image as an employer able to easier to attract and retain employees than an organization with negative image. Organizations actions and activities like good public relations, public service like, charity, contraction and development roads, public parks, hospitals education and schools help earn image or goodwill for organization.

4. Political-Social- Legal Environment

Different government controls forbidding separation in contracting and work have coordinate effect on enlistment practices.

5. Unemployment Rate

The Element that influence the availability of applicants is the economy growth rate . At the point when the organization isn't making new jobs, there is frequently oversupply of qualified work which thusly prompts unemployment.

6. Competitors

The recruitment policies and procedure an of the competitors also affect the recruitment function of the organizations. Time to time the organizations have to change their recruitment policies and manuals according to the policies being followed by the competitors.

Recruitment is one of the main departments which place the right candidates to the right job. The recruiters should identify the best candidates from different sources and job sites. Recruiters have to identify the problems faced during recruitment and find an alternative to make work efficiently which can fulfil recruitment goal on time .

Definition of Selection

According to Harold Koontz, "Selection is the process of choosing from the candidates, from within the organization or from outside, the most suitable person for the current position or for the future positions."

Dale Yoder said, "Selection is the process by which candidates for employment are divided into classes those who will be offered employment and those who will not."

David and Robbins said, "Selection process is a managerial decision-making process as to predict which job applicants will be successful if hired."

According to R.M. Hodgetts, "Selection is the process in which an enterprise chooses the applicants who best meet the criteria for the available positions."

Selection is the process of choosing from a group of applicants those individuals best suited for a particular position.

Most managers recognize that employee selection is one of their most difficult, and most important, business decisions.

This process involves making a judgment -not about the applicant, but about the fit between the applicant and the job by considering knowledge, skills and abilities and other characteristics required to perform the job Selection procedures are not carried out through standard pattern and steps in this.

The process can vary from organization to organization some steps performed and considered important by one organization can be skipped by other organization.

Personnel Selection is the methodical placement of individuals into jobs. Its impact on the organization is realized when employees achieve years or decades of service to the employer.

The process of selection follows a methodology to collect information about an individual in order to determine if that individual should be employed. The methodology used should not violate any laws regarding personnel selection.

Steps in Selection Process

The selection process typically begins with the preliminary interview; next, candidates complete the application for employment.

They progress through a series of selection tests, the employment interview, and reference and background checks. The successful applicant receives a company physical examination and is employed if the results are satisfactory.

Several external and internal factors impact the selection process, and the manager must take them into account in making selection decisions.

Typically selection process consists of the following steps but it is not necessary that all organization go through all these steps as per the requirement of the organization some steps can be skipped while performing the selection process.

1. Initial Screening.
2. Completion of the Application Form.
3. Employment Tests.
4. Job Interview.
5. Conditional Job Offer.
6. Background Investigation.
7. Medical Examination.
8. Permanent Job Offer.

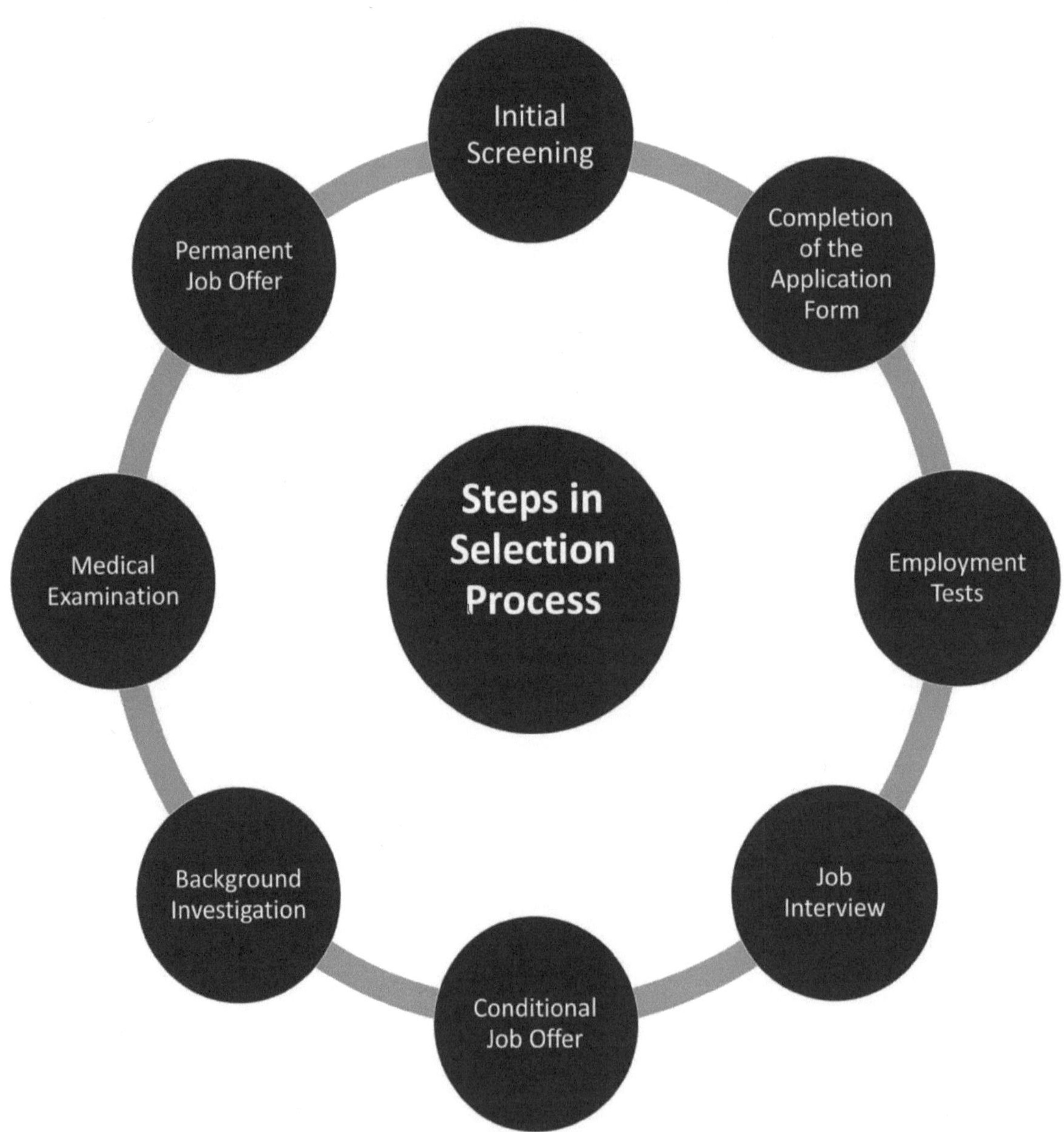

Steps in Selection Process

1. Initial Screening

The selection process often begins with an initial screening of applicants to remove individuals who obviously do not meet the position requirements.

At this stage, a few straight forward questions are asked. An applicant may obviously be unqualified to fill the advertised position, but be well qualified to work in other open positions.

The Purpose of Screening is to decrease the number of applicants being considered for selection.

Sources utilized in the screening effort

Personal Resume presented with the job application is considered a source of information that can be used for the initial screening process. It mainly includes information in the following areas:

- Employment & education history.
- Evaluation of character.
- Evaluation of job performance.

Advantages of Successful Screening

If the screening effort is successful, those applicants that do not meet the minimum required qualifications will not move to the next stage in the selection process. Companies utilizing expensive selection procedures put more effort into screening to reduce costs.

2. Completion of the Application Form

Application Blank is a formal record of an individual's application for employment. The next step in the selection process may involve having the prospective employee complete an application for employment.

This may be as brief as requiring only an applicant's name, address, and telephone number. In general terms, the application form gives a job-performance-related synopsis of applicants' life, skills and accomplishments.

The specific type of information may vary from firm to firm and even by job type within an organization. Application forms are a good way to quickly collect verifiable and fairly accurate historical data from the candidate.

3. Employment Tests

Personnel testing is a valuable way to measure individual characteristics.

Hundreds of tests have been developed to measure various dimensions of behavior. The tests measure mental abilities, knowledge, physical abilities, personality, interest, temperament, and other attitudes and behaviors.

Evidence suggests that the use of tests is becoming more prevalent for assessing an applicant's qualifications and potential for success. Tests are used more in the public sector than in the private sector and in medium-sized and large companies than in small companies.

Large organizations are likely to have trained specialists to run their testing programs.

Advantages of using tests

Selection testing can be a reliable and accurate means of selecting qualified candidates from a pool of applicants.

As with all selection procedures, it is important to identify the essential functions of each job and determine the skills needed to perform them.

Potential Problems using Selection tests

Selection tests may accurately predict an applicant's ability to perform the job, but they are less successful in indicating the extent to which the individual will want to perform it.

Another potential problem, related primarily to personality tests and interest inventories, has to do with applicants honesty. Also, there is the problem of test anxiety.

Applicants often become quite anxious when confronting yet another hurdle that might eliminate them from consideration.

4. Job Interview

An interview is a goal-oriented conversation in which the interviewer and applicant exchange information. The employment interview is especially significant because the applicants who reach this stage are considered to be the most promising candidates.

Interview Planning

Interview planning is essential to effective employment interviews.

The physical location of the interview should be both pleasant and private, providing for a minimum of interruptions. The interviewer should possess a pleasant personality, empathy and the ability to listen and communicate effectively.

He or she should become familiar with the applicant's qualifications by reviewing the data collected from other selection tools. In preparing for the interview, a job profile should be developed based on the job description.

Content of the Interview

The specific content of employment interviews varies greatly by an organization and the level of the job concerned.

1. **Occupational experience:** Exploring an individual's occupational experience requires determining the applicant's skills, abilities, and willingness to handle responsibility.
2. **Academic achievement:** In the absence of significant work experience, a person's academic background takes on greater importance.
3. **Interpersonal skills:** If an individual cannot work well with other employees, chances for success are slim. This is especially true in today's world with increasing emphasis being placed on the use of teams.
4. **Personal qualities:** Personal qualities normally observed during the interview include physical appearance, speaking ability, vocabulary, poise, adaptability, and assertiveness.
5. **Organizational fit:** A hiring criterion that is not prominently mentioned in the literature is organizational fit. Organizational fit is ill-defined but refers to management's perception of the degree to which the prospective employee will fit in with, for example, the firm's culture or value system.

5. Conditional Job Offer

Conditional job offer means a tentative job offer that becomes permanent after certain conditions are met.

If a job applicant has passed each step of the selection process so far, a conditional job offer is usually made.

In essence, the conditional job offer implies that if everything checks out – such as passing a certain medical, physical or substance abuse test – the conditional nature of the job offer will be removed and the offer will be permanent.

6. Background Investigation

Background Investigation is intended to verify that information on the application form is correct and accurate.

This step is used to check the accuracy of application form through former employers and references. Verification of education and legal status to work, credit history and criminal record are also made.

Personal reference checks may provide additional insight into the information furnished by the applicant and allow verification of its accuracy.

Past behavior is the best predictor of future behavior. It is important to gain as much information as possible about past behavior to understand what kinds of behavior one can expect in the future.

Knowledge about attendance problems, insubordination issues, theft, or other behavioral problems can certainly help one avoid hiring someone who is likely to repeat those behaviors.

Background investigations primarily seek data from references supplied by the applicant including his or her previous employers. The intensity of background investigations depends on the level of responsibility inherent in the position to be filled.

Common sources of background information include:

- References are provided by the applicant and are usually very positive.
- Former employers should be called to confirm the candidate's work record and to obtain their performance appraisal.
- Educational accomplishments can be verified by asking for transcripts.
- Legal status to work.
- Credit references, if job-related.
- Criminal records can be checked by third-party investigators.
- Background checks are conducted by third-party investigators.
- Online searches as simple as "Google" search of a candidate can turn up information on press releases or news items about a candidate that was left off the application or resume.

7. Medical/Physical Examination

After the decision has been made to extend a job offer, the next phase of the selection process involves the completion of a medical/physical examination.

This is an examination to determine an applicant's physical fitness for essential job performance.

Typically, a job offer is contingent on successfully passing this examination.

For example, firefighters must perform activities that require a certain physical condition. Whether it is climbing a ladder, lugging a water-filled four-inch hose or carrying an injured victim, these individuals must demonstrate that they are fit for the job.

8. Permanent Job Offer

Individuals who perform successfully in the preceding steps are now considered eligible to receive the employment offer. The actual hiring decision should be made by the manager in the department where the vacancy exists.

Notification to Candidates

The selection process results should be made known to candidates—successful and unsuccessful—as soon as possible.

Any delay may result in the firm losing a prime candidate, as top prospects often have other employment options. As a matter of courtesy and good public relations, the unsuccessful candidates should also be promptly notified.

Ways of Making an Effective Employee Selection

All companies, irrespective of size, make hiring mistakes, but here are few tips experts /suggest to help avoid making them.

Determine the criteria a candidate must meet

Before filling a position, the HR manager of a company must clearly define the skills, experience, character, 'educational background, work experience, technical skills and competencies, they must possess.

Hiring without testing

Skill testing is a must. Every job has some form of measurable, objective performance standard. Identify it and test for it.

There are tests that can indicate if a job candidate meets the required criteria. With these pre-hire screening tools, a recruiter can test the knowledge of potential hires before they are extended an offer.

Hiring after the first interview

It is important to have several interviews with the same person — and not to hire from one interview. The person may not present the same later, and HR manager may get fresh insights from different meetings.

Underestimating the unemployed.

A person who does not have a job at the Vnoment may be the right fit for the position. They are plenty of good talent out there that are not hired.

Poor or no reference checking

It is important to know how to conduct a detailed 'reference check. A proper reference check verifies job skills and the behavioral fit in which the person operates. It is essential to conduct an extensive background investigation and reference checks.

Avoid hiring out of desperation

Too many hiring decisions are made out of operation. The following scenarios occur repeatedly; a key manager quits and must be replaced now; rapid growth forces a company to fill positions without enough forethought; programmers are so scarce that anyone will do.

If we hire employees in haste, we may find out later that the new recruits are not trustworthy or competent.

If an HR manager is unable to conduct a thorough, timely hiring process, hire a temporary or leased employee or borrow an employee from another company.

Watch out for fascination

A series of surveys have revealed that during the hiring process, most interviewers made their decision-up or down within the first 10 minutes of the interview.

They then spent the next 50 minutes internally justifying that decision. We buy cars in the same way.

First, we choose the car we want to buy from an emotional standpoint and then search for objective data to justify that emotional decision.

We all know that facts tell, but emotions sell. The recruiter can guard against obsession by having coworkers' interview prospects, having group interviews, and by conducting follow-up interviews.

Carefully evaluate candidates recommended by employees and associates.

Just because someone recommends a person they think would be highly capable for a particular position doesn't mean that person is qualified.

We have seen many occasions where someone was hired without going through the usual evaluation process simply because they were recommended by another employee or colleague Follow the usual channels and requirements when anyone-no matter how highly recommended-seeks to work for the organization.

Do not blindly promote from within

It is widely believed that the HR manager should recruit employees from within the organization. The best performers are not necessarily always the most qualified candidates for a specific job. This is especially true when promoting to the management level.

Simply because someone is particularly adept at handling a certain function doesn't mean they are capable of managing others. It is important to remember the Peter Principle.

It is a concept in management theory in which the selection of a candidate for a position is based on their performance in the current role rather than on their abilities relevant to the intended role.

Peter suggests that people will tend to be promoted until they reach their "position of incompetence".

One's career may cripple after such a promotion. Promoting solely from within can create inbreeding and stagnate creativity.

To guard against these pitfalls, companies should consider filling at least one-third of all positions involving promotions with people from outside the organization.

Common Mistakes in the Selection of Employees

If workers are carefully selected, the problems of employee discipline will be negligible.

Consequently, hiring employees is a major part of the success of every company. Colin, (2011) and Fraser (2012) identified some common mistakes that might occur while hiring new employees.

Organizations today are experiencing high rates of employee turnover, wrongful hiring claims, gender discrimination, political consideration, regionalism, workplace violence; and employee theft, etc.

Hiring a wrong person may aggravate such risk.

The wrong person is under-qualified, insubordinate, and detrimental to the entire firm. Indeed, the seeds of many failed employee-employer relationships are planted during the hiring process.

The wrong person may be an unavoidable liability for the organization. The wrong person can do a lot of damage to the organization. Hiring mistakes can be more costly.

These mistakes can include the cost of termination, replacement and productivity loss. They can impact the organization's bottom line as well as the morale and productivity of other employees.

Selecting the right people is a key leverage point to support and drive an organization's growth and development.

But selecting the right person is not an easy task. Many mistakes may occur while selecting employees. The cost associated with the making such a mistake are tremendous.

Both dismissal and turnover are costly.

The best way to reduce turnover is to make the right selection decision in the beginning of the entire process. Selecting the right people is crucial to an organization's success.

How can HR manager make sure that he or she is not making the top hiring mistakes?

Colin (2011) says, "It's important to get your hiring right the first time and encourages employers to take steps to reduce the likelihood of costly hiring mistakes".

However, the following mistakes are identified in the selection process of an employee:

Poor listening

Few recruiters do not pay full attention to the candidate. In fact /following the 80: 20 rule, the 80% needs to come from the applicant.

The interviewer should listen 80% of the time.

Recruiters listen to the candidate's words

They should pay more attention to the body language, posture, eye contact: essentially all the non-verbal communication cues.

About 93% of all communication is nonverbal, so being attuned to the multitude of nonverbal cues provides an interviewer with much richer information about the candidate (McMurray, R. N., 1990).

They should read and observe the personality of the applicants.

For example, voice quality is important for a candidate to become a teacher, in addition to his academic qualification. Recruiters should talk less and listen more.

Questions are not purposeful

This is due to a lack of preparation. If recruiters /have benchmarked the job and prepared a list of questions in advance, then they cannot go wrong.

Recruiters should get prepared both for the basic and follow-up questions.

A review of the job specification and employee specification may help the interviewer prepare specific questions. They should build rapport with the interviewee. The burden to establish rapport falls on the interviewer.

Recruiters do not know what they are looking for

The recruiters may lack in / preparation. So make a list of all the hard skills as well as soft skills (personality traits and personal values) that employers need for the employee.

Jot down any additional demands the job requires, such as lots of overtime, travel and set hours. The recruiter must know exactly what they are looking for, they are more likely to get it. Like most decision making, employee selection is fundamentally emotional.

Therefore, it is important to define and prioritize the Critical Success Factors for the job in advance.

This enables clear thinking to establish a specific position profile. Yes, it takes time, but it is an effective use of time versus “shooting in the dark.”.

Use the gut feels the approach

Experience and intuition are important no doubt but do /not ignore the selection process. Have procedures in place which will assist a recruiter in making the right choice, such as testing, pre-interview questionnaires, psychometric assessments, etc.

It is important to verify and check all information provided in the resume to make sure that nothing is given wrong.

Be open to the possibility that some of them might not be totally honest and are bending the truth to get the job. It is very common for applicants to paint a much brighter picture on their resumes so this makes testing extra important.

Time and work under pressure

Recruiters spend too little time on hiring and make /take too long to look for a replacement. They should understand that the costs of hiring are nothing as compared to turnover costs.

Don't meet the candidate only once. Create opportunities for other managers to meet the applicant as well and hear what they have to say. It is very important to get the whole picture and see whether the applicant will be an overall good fit for the company.

Go with the flow

Most interviewers do not take control of the interview. HR /managers must remember, it is his interview. He not candidate-set the process, timing, roles, pace, and questioning.

Take candidates at their word

Do not settle for vague general responses just because you want to be polite. Let the candidate know at the beginning of the interview that as an HR manager, your goal is to fully and- specifically understand his/her capabilities.

Oblivious to the legal

This may not prevent HR managers from making the right /selection decision, but it will increase the company's liabilities to solve this problem, the HR manager must know the law, train employees and enforce the law in his selection process.

Ignorance is no excuse.

Where Recruitment Ends Selection Starts

Recruitment involves attracting and obtaining as many applications as possible from eligible job seekers. Recruitment is the process of finding and attracting capable applicants for employment.

The process begins when new recruits are sought and ends when their applications are submitted. The result is a pool of applicants from which new employees are selected.

Selection is the process of differentiating between applicants in order to identify and hire those with a greater likelihood of success in a job. Though some selection methods can be used within the organization for promotion or transfer, in this case, the statement of the question is not correct.

But when the selection of applicants from outside the organization has occurred then the given statement in the question is correct.

Recruitment and relation are the two crucial steps in the HR process and are often used interchangeably. There is however a fine distinction between the two steps.

While recruitment refers to the process of identifying and encouraging prospective employees to apply for jobs, the selection is concerned with picking the right candidates from the pool of applicants which are obtained during the recruitment process.

So in this case selection is derived from after completing the recruitment process. Recruitment is said to be positive in its approach as it seeks to attract as many candidates as possible.

Selection, on the other hand, is negative in its application in as much as it seeks to element as many unqualified applicants as possible in order to identify the right candidates from the pool.

So in the recruitment and selection process; recruitment is the first step and selection is the second steps or final step.

In conclusion, we can say "When recruitment ends selection to start.

Selection, Recruitment and Job Analysis Relationship

Job analysis

Job analysis is the process of collecting job-related information. Such information helps in the preparation of job description and job specification.

A job is a collection of tasks that can be performed by a single employee to contribute to the production of some product or service provided by the organization.

Each job has certain ability requirements as well as certain rewards associated with it. Job analysis is the process used to identify these requirements.

Job analysis involves the following steps:

1. Collection and recording job information.
2. Checking the job information for accuracy.
3. Writing job descriptions based on the information
4. Using the information to determine the skills, abilities, and knowledge that are required on the job.
5. Upgrading the information from time to time.

Job analysis has an impact on all foundations of HRM. Job analysis, if properly has done will enhance the effectiveness of all HR activities.

It benefits the organization in the following ways:

1. Laying the foundation for human resources planning.
2. Laying the foundation for employee hiring.
3. Laying the foundation for training and development.
4. Laying the foundation for performance appraisal.
5. Laying the foundation for salary and wage fixation.
6. Laying the foundation for safety and health.

Recruitment

Recruitment involves attracting and obtaining as many applications as possible from eligible job seekers. It is the process of finding and attracting capable applicants for employment. The process begins when new recruits are sought and ends when their applications are submitted. The result is a pool of applicants from which new employees are selected.

Selection

Selection is the process of differentiating between applicants in order to identify and hire those with a greater likelihood of success in a job.

Recruitment and selection are the two crucial steps in the HR process and are often used interchangeably.

There is, however, a fine distinction between the two steps.

While recruitment refers to the process of identifying and encouraging prospective employees to apply for jobs then the selection is concerned with picking the right candidates from a pool of applicants.

From the above discussion, we can find a relationship between the recruitment and selection i.e. recruitment is the precondition for the selection of an employee for the organization.

The relationship between "Job analysis" and "Recruitment and Selection" is i.e. job analysis is the foundation of recruitment and selection for selecting a qualified and capable employee as required for performing the job accurately.

CHAPTER THREE

Human Resource Development

Human Resource Development (HRD) Concept

Human Resource Development (HRD) is the framework for helping employees develop their personal and organizational skills, knowledge, and abilities. Human Resource Development includes such opportunities as employee training, employee career development, performance management and development, coaching, mentoring, succession planning, key employee identification, tuition assistance, and organization development.

The focus of all aspects of Human Resource Development is on developing the most superior workforce so that the organization and individual employees can accomplish their work goals in service to customers.

Human Resource Development can be formal such as in classroom training, a college course, or an organizational planned change effort. Or, Human Resource Development can be informal as in employee coaching by a manager. Healthy organizations believe in Human Resource Development and cover all of these bases.

Planned Human Resource Development is critical to the achievement of a skilled and efficient workforce. Developing people to their full potential will contribute significantly to an agency achieving its business outcomes. Proper planning takes into account whole of government, agency and individual needs. It will ensure that developmental activities reflect the agency's strategic direction and maximise the learning outcomes for individuals. The Guideline provides principles on which public sector agencies can base the development of policies and practices to ensure the planned provision of human resource development.

Objectives of Human Resources Development

Four Objectives of Human Resources Development are :

(A) To Provide A Comprehensive Platform For The Development Of Human Resources In The Organization

(B) To provide a climate for employees to discover, develop, and use their knowledge for the betterment of organization

(C) To retain, attract and motivate the talented employees

(D) To facilitate systematic generation of information.

(A) To provide a comprehensive platform for the development of Human Resources In the organisation:

Every HRD programmed starts with providing a framework within the organisation so that employees develop on their own-on the job.

Employees would be given freedom to express their feeling with the superiors. The superiors also respect the feelings of employees and suggest them (not in a critical tone) so that they develop.

(B) To provide a climate for employees to discover, develop, and use their knowledge for the betterment of organisation:

Another basic objective of HRD programmer is to create a work climate in the organisation whereby the employees contribute their best in the organisation. Every employee, in an HRD programmer, is given full freedom to exhibit his skills, talents and knowledge for the benefit of enterprise. Innovative ideas and schemes would be encouraged and appreciated in the organisation.

(C) To retain, attract and motivate the talented employees:

An organisation concluding HRD programme has the tendency of attracting and retaining the talented employees.

People would get an impression that organisation is providing a convenient platform to fully stretch their capacities and the talented people would get motivated when their intelligence and knowledge get recognized and acknowledged by the organisation. Organisations lacking in HRD programmes would least motivate the productive and effective employees.

(D) To facilitate systematic generation of information:

An HRD programme facilitates the organisation to get access to information on human resources for planning, development, placement, career planning and succession planning.

History

The term HRD has been growing at a very fast pace in the recent past. But the formal introduction of the concept was done by Prof. Len Nadler in 1969 in American Society for Training and Development Conference. In India, Larsen & Toubro was the first company to design and implement this concept in 1975 among the private sector companies with an objective of facilitating growth of employees, especially people at the lower levels. Among the public sector government company, it was BHEL which introduced this concept in 1980.

The intended purpose of human resources development efforts is to gain a competitive advantage in the market place through a superior workforce. There are several trends from which the concept of HRD has emerged. Let us look into those trends more closely by examining the transformation of personnel function from one stage to another in a chronological sequence.

The evolution of human resource development can be easily understood in the following chronological Sequence:

1. The Commodity Concept:

Human resource was referred as 'a commodity' to be ought and sold. Wages were decided on the basis of demand and supply forces. Government also did not care much about the work force at that time.

2. The Factor of Production Concept:

Labour is treated as any other factor of production, viz; money, material, land, etc.

3. The Goodwill Concept:

Welfare measures like safety, first aid, lunch room, rest room etc. These measures proved to be a source of boosting up the morale of workers and enhancing their performance.

4. The Paternalistic Concept:

Management must assume a fatherly and protective attitude towards employers. Paternalism does not mean merely providing benefits but it signifies to satisfy various needs of employees just as parents meet the requirements of the children.

5. The Humanitarian Concept:

To improve the productivity, physical, social and psychological needs of workers must be fulfilled. Elton Mayo and some other along with him stated that money is less a factor in determining output, than group standards, group incentives and security. The Organization is a social system that has both economic and social dimensions.

6. The Human Resource Concept:

Employees are the most valuable assets of an organization. There should be a conscious effort to realize organizational goals by satisfying needs and aspirations of employees.

7. The Emerging Concept of Human Resource Development (HRD):

Employees should be accepted as partners in the progress of a company. They should have a feeling that the organization is their own. To this end, managers must offer better quality of working life and provide opportunities to people to exploit their potential fully. There should be opportunities for self-fulfilment in one's work.

Significance of Human Resource Development (HRD)

Human resource is needed to be developed as per the change in the external environment of the organization, hence, HRD helps to adopt such changes through the development of existing human resource in terms of skill and knowledge.

The purpose of HR development is to provide the 'coaching' needed to strengthen and grow the knowledge, skills, and abilities that an employee already has. The goal of development and training is to make employees even better at what they do.

The importance or significance of HRD can be explained as follows:

1. HRD expands capable HR

HRD develops the skills and knowledge of individual; hence, it helps to provide competent and efficient HR as per the job requirement. To develop employment's skill and competencies, different training and development programs are launched.

2. HRD builds prospect for Career Development

HRD helps to grasp the career development opportunities through the development of human skills and knowledge. Career development consists of personal development efforts through a proper match between training and development opportunities with employee's need.

3. Employ Promise

Trained and efficient employees are committed towards their jobs which is possible through HRD. If employees are provided with proper training and development opportunities, they will feel committed to the work and the organization.

4. Job Fulfillment

When people in the organization are well oriented and developed, they show a higher degree of commitment in an actual workplace. This inspires them for better performance, which ultimately leads to job satisfaction.

5. Transform Management

HRD facilitates planning and management of change in an organization. It also manages conflicts through improved labor management relation. It develops organizational health, culture, and environment which lead to change management.

6. Opportunities for Training and Development

Training and development programs are tools of HRD. They provide an opportunity for employee's development by matching training needs with the organizational requirement. Moreover, HRD facilitates integrated growth of employees through training and development activities.

7. Performance development

HRD develops necessary skills and abilities required to perform organizational activities. As a result of which, employees can contribute to better performance in an organization. This leads to greater organizational effectiveness.

Principles of Human Resource Development (HRD)

Following are some of the principles of human resource development (HRD), which must be kept in mind while framing a Human Resource Development system so as to have a proper and regular development of the human resource in an organization.

Principle of Development of Organizational Capability:

An ideal HRD system should be based on the principle of overall development of employees and the organization as a whole. The capabilities include overall development of the work force in all aspects, may it be technical, physical, psychological or moral development in an organized manner.

Principle of Potential Maximization:

HRD system must enable their employees to identify their hidden potential and make them competent enough to exploit their talent in an optimum manner so that they could contribute their efforts in attaining organizational goals.

Principle of Autonomy Maximization:

Autonomy is the degree of independence given to employees at work so that they could be able to tackle responsibility to some extent of what they are capable of handling. A proper HRD system must provide certain level of autonomy to its employees enabling them of handling duties on their own.

Principle of Maximum delegation:

Delegation of responsibilities means sharing responsibilities of authorities with subordinates so that a cohesive and a congenial environment could be developed in an organization.

Principle of Participative Decision-making:

Participation of subordinates must be encouraged by top level managers in an ideal HRD system to create a comfortable working atmosphere where workers are free to discuss their ideas and always welcomed for suggestions.

Principle of Change Management:

Change is the only permanent thing in this universe but usually people resists change. To beat the competition an organization and its human resource should be as much flexible in getting itself adapt to the changing scenario of 21st century. A good HRD system must attempt to strike a balance between the organizational culture and the changing culture.

Principle of Periodic Review:

Review and renewal of HRD functions like training and development, career planning and development, performance and potential appraisal, counseling, etc. of employees should take place regularly in an organization at certain periodic intervals.

Human resource development is a process of developing the workforce extending their services to any organization by enhancing their knowledge and skills through proper training and guidance. It ultimately aims at achieving the organizational goals by combating them with the goals of the individuals working in an organization. There are certain objectives for implementing HRD in any organization which aims at developing

- the capabilities of each employees as individuals;
- the capabilities of each individual employee in relation to his/her present job;
- the capabilities of each individual employee in relation to his/her expected future role;
- the superior-subordinate (dyadic) relationship;
- a cohesive and congenial atmosphere of working;
- collaboration among different units of an organization;
- to develop the constructive mind and overall personality of employees;

- the organization's overall health and self-renewing capabilities which in turn increase the organizational capabilities in a comprehensive manner;
- to humanize the work in an organization; and
- to ensure better quality work, higher productivity and higher profits.

CHAPTER FOUR

Motivation

Motivation is the process that initiates, guides, and maintains goal-oriented behaviors. It is what causes you to act, whether it is getting a glass of water to reduce thirst or reading a book to gain knowledge.

Motivation involves the biological, emotional, social, and cognitive forces that activate behavior. In everyday usage, the term "motivation" is frequently used to describe *why* a person does something. It is the driving force behind human actions.

Motivation doesn't just refer to the factors that activate behaviors; it also involves the factors that direct and maintain these goal-directed actions (though such motives are rarely directly observable). As a result, we often have to infer the reasons why people do the things that they do based on observable behaviors.

Motivation is an important factor which encourages persons to give their best performance and help in reaching organizational goals. A strong positive motivation will enable the increased output of employees but a negative motivation will reduce their performance. A key element in personnel management is motivation. According to Likert, " It s the core of management which shows that every human being gives him a sense of worth in face-to-face groups which are most important to him. A supervisor should strive to treat individuals with dignity and recognition of their personal worth."

Employee Motivation

Motivation is the most essential part of the work life of an employee. It inspires individuals for putting in their efforts towards the attainment of the organizational goals.

The motivational tools should be formulated by taking into consideration the fact that individuals join the organization because they feel that their personal goals would be satisfied by getting associated with the organization.

Motivation is required in every sphere of organizational life, as it helps in building the zeal and interest among the employees to pursue organizational goals. It also increases the efficiency of the employees.

Employee Motivation – Meaning and Definitions

Employee Motivation definitions by Michael J. Jucius, Dale Beach, Mc Farland, Koontz and O'Donnell, Edwin B. Flippo, Scott, Dubin, Lillis.

Motivate is a "Latin word" meaning "to move" human motives are internalised goals within individuals. We can define motive as a factor that makes a person act a particular way. It is an inner impulse causing man to action. Motive is defined as an inner state of our mind that energizes, activates or moves and directs or channelises our behavior towards goals. A motive is the mainspring of human action. A motive is the active form of a desire, craving or need, a motive works towards a cherished goal.

It is goal-directed, it in itself is invisible. Motivation is the process which influences people to act. The process involves need drives and goals. Motivation is always internal. It is externalised through behaviour. Motivation-behaviour-goal is called the cycle of Motivation. The cycle continues till the goal is achieved. It can be defined as the willingness to exert towards accomplishment of some goal. It focuses inner drives that activate or move an individual to action.

The force of motivation lies within the mind. It is a dynamic force setting a person into motion and action. A man is motivated or set into action either by extrinsic rewards and punishments or by intrinsic incentives. Motivation is, thus, an art of stimulating people to take desired course of action. Some people may be motivated by the rewards while others are self-motivated. Thus motivation is a process to get the needs of the people realised with a view to induce them to work.

Indeed, motivation is nothing but an action of inducement. The skill of motivating the people is the life blood of an organisation. Hence it is important to understand people and the way to handle this dynamic human resource, so that people work to the utmost ability that too with interest. Psychologists define motivation as that which arouses behaviour, sustains it and channelises the behaviour into a specific course.

Motivation is the process of creating organisational conditions which will impel emphasis to strive to attain organisational goals. Psychologists generally agree that all behaviour, sustains it and channelises the behaviour into a specific course. Motivation is the process of creating organisational conditions which will impel emphasis to strive to attain organisational goals.

Psychologists generally agree that all behaviours are motivated and that people have reasons for doing the things they do or for behaving in the manner that they do. In other words, all human behaviour is designed to achieve certain goals and objectives. Such goal directed behaviour revolves around the desire for need satisfaction.

We may define motivation as, "a willingness to expend energy to achieve as goal or reward. It is a force that activates dormant energies and sets in motion the action of the people. It is a function that kindles a burning passion for action among the human beings of an organisation".

Here are some important definitions of motivation:

Michael J. Jucius – "Motivation is the act of stimulating one or oneself to get a desired course of action to push the right button to get desired results".

Dale Beach – "Motivation can be defined as willingness to expend energy to achieve a goal or a reward".

Mc Farland – Motivation refers to the way in which urges, drives, desires, aspirations, striving or needs, direct, control or explain the behaviour of human beings.

Koontz and O'Donnell – "Motivation is a general term applying to the entire class of drives, desires, needs, wishes and similar force that induce an individual or a group of people to work".

Edwin B. Flippo – "Motivation is the process of attempting to influence others to do their work through the possibility of gain or reward".

Scott – "Motivation means a process of stimulating people to action to accomplishing desired goals".

Dubin – "Motivation is the complex of force starting and keeping person at work in an organisation".

Lillis – "Motivation is the stimulation of any emotion or desire operating upon ones will and prompting or driving one to action".

J. E. Rosenz Weig and F. K. Kast – "Motivation is an inspiration process which impels the members of the team to accomplish the desired goals."

S. Zedck and M. Blood – "Motivation is a pre-disposition to act in a specified goal directed way."

The Encyclopedia of Management observes – "Motivation refers to the degree of readiness of an organism to pursue some designated goal, and implies the determination of the nature and locus of the forces, including the degree of readiness."

Tolman observes, "More specifically, the term motivation has been called an intervening variable" Intervening variables are internal and psychological process which are not directly observable and which, in turn, account for behaviour."

Thus motivation consists of the three interacting and interdependent elements of needs, drives and goals. Needs are the deficiencies and are created whenever there is a physiological or psychological imbalance. Drives or Motives are set to alleviate needs. These are action oriented and provided an energizing thrust towards goal accomplishment. They are the very heart of motivational process.

Goals are anything which will alleviate a need and reduce a drive. There are some facts about motivation need, such as – (i) Motivation is a hypothetical concept which is defined in terms of antecedent conditions and consequent behaviour, (ii) Motivation is an intervening variable for it cannot be seen, heard or felt and can only be inferred from behaviour. For instance, motives such as hunger, sex, power and achievement cannot be seen. Restlessness, walking, running, eating or talking or winning a new friend can be observed.

Above definitions reveal the following characteristics of motivation:

1. It is an Internal Instinct or it is a Psychological Concept:

Motivation refers to a feeling within individuals. It is an inner state that energizes, activates or moves and directs or channelises behaviour towards goals. All human behaviour is designed to achieve certain goals and objectives.

Such a goal directed behaviour revolves around the desire for need satisfaction. The need setup drives to accomplish goals. Motivation consists of the three interacting and interdependent elements of needs, drives and goals.

2. Man is Motivated as a Whole and Not in Part:

It is not possible that a part of a man is motivated but whole man is motivated. A person's basic needs determine to a great extent, what he will try to do at any given time. Needs are the deficiencies and are created whenever there is a physiological or psychological imbalance.

Motivation represents an unsatisfied need which creates a state of tension or dis-equilibrium, causing individual to move in a goal directed pattern towards restoring a state of equilibrium by satisfying the need. Motivation implies any emotion or desire which so conditions ones will that the individual is properly led into action.

3. Motivation is Always Goal Oriented:

Goals and motivates are inseparable. Man's behaviour itself is goal oriented. Man works to achieve some goals or objectives. Motivation has a profound influence on human behaviour. It directs human behaviour towards the goals. As soon as his goal is achieved he would be two longer, interested in work.

Therefore it is essential for management to know his goal to push him to work. In simple words motivation causes goal oriented behaviour.

4. Motivation is a Continuous or Endless Process:

The goals of the individual and the organisation can be achieved through stimulation workers towards productive performance called motivational process and it is a continuous process. Man is a social being and has unlimited wants, needs, desires, which induce him to work. If one need is satisfied, it loses its power as a motivator and at the same time another need arises. Needs, wants are innumerable and cannot be satisfied at one time. Satisfaction of needs is an unending process, therefore the process of motivation is a continuous one.

5. Motivation can be Positive or Negative:

Workers can be motivated either positively or negatively. Positive motivation, sometimes called "anxiety reducing motivation" or the "carrot approach", offer something valuable to the workers, for instance, pay, praise, appreciation bonus, promotion etc. for better performance from them. Punishments, fear, removing security of job, demotion, fines, cut in pay, dismissal, retrenchment etc. are the examples of negative motivation methods where people work in fear.

Employee Motivation Features

The ultimate goal of every organisation is to increase its productivity. Hence, motivation of employees at all levels is the most critical function of management. Motivated employee produce a goal directed behaviour with his own generator. Outside simulation is not needed to such employee again and again. Inspire of outside forces he is driven himself.

The analysis of various definition and following on motivation reveals.

The following features of motivation are:

1. Motivation is an internal feeling. The urge, desires, aspirations, striving or needs of human being, which are internal influence human behaviour.

For example – People may have the urge or desire for possessing a motorbike, comfortable house, reputation in the society. These urges are internal to an individual.

2. Motivation produces goal directed behaviour for example – The promotion in the job may be given to employee with the objective of improving his performance.

3. Motivation can be either positive or negative. Positive motivation provides positive towards like increase in pay, promotion, recognition etc. Negative motivation uses negative means like punishment, stopping increments, threatening etc.

4. Motivation is a complex process- As the individuals are heterogeneous in their expectations, perceptions and reactions, any type of motivation may not uniform effect for all the members.

Objectives of Motivation:

1. To Create Conditions:

Main basic objective of motivation is to create conditions in which people are willing to work with zeal, initiative, interest and enthusiasm with a high moral satisfaction personal as well as group. Motivation, as well creates feeling or responsibility and loyalty. This ultimately results indiscipline. Naturally the workers feel pride and confident towards achievement of organisational goals effectively.

2. To Stimulate Employee Growth:

Motivational techniques are utilised to stimulate employee growth. Clarence Francis rightly said that "You can buy a man's time, you can buy a man's physical presence at a given place, you can even buy a measured number of skilled muscular motions per hour or day, but you cannot buy enthusiasm, you cannot buy initiative, you cannot buy loyalty, you cannot buy devotion of hearts, minds and souls. You have to earn these things." Motivation helps management in winning those that cannot be bought.

Managers believe that motivation is one of the most important factors in managing human resources today.

3. To Achieve Organisational Goals:

Predetermined objectives and goals of any organisation can be achieved by willful as well as efficient work by the work force. Motivation only, can make the workforce to stand to expected standards and efficiency. It, therefore, is a basic duty of every manager to motivate his subordinates for the attainment of predetermined organisational goals and objectives.

4. For Better Utilisation of Human and Non-Human Resources:

It is the duty of every manager to utilise both human and non-human resources in the best possible way. If managers motivate the employees continuously, they will automatically ensure best utilisation of human resources. If human resources are timely and properly motivated, they, in turn utilise the non-human resources properly. Through motivation there will be better utilisation of resources and worker's abilities and capabilities.

5. For Job Satisfaction:

Higher motivation leads to job satisfaction of workers which can reduce absenteeism, turnover and labour unrest.

6. For Better Industrial Relations:

If management is successful in understanding the motives or needs of the workers and provides an environment in which appropriate incentives are available for their need satisfaction, it leads to better industrial relations between management and workers. It also will increase efficiency and effectiveness of the organisation. Motivation will also foster team spirit among the workers and increase their loyalty to the organisation.

Importance of Motivation

In the directing process, motivation is one of the important elements. By motivating people, the manager guides people's actions in the desired direction so as to enable him to achieve the organizational objectives. For performing any job, two important things are necessary, viz., will to work and ability to work. The importance of motivation lies in converting this ability to work into the will to work. For performing any job, there is a need for both, viz., the ability and willingness to work.

Without willingness, ability to work is of no use. Hence, there is a need for motivating a person to do his job. Performance depends on ability and willingness and in turn, willingness depends on motivation. It can be expressed in a formula – Performance = Ability x Motivation.

The following points highlight the importance of motivation:

(1) Maximum utilization of factors of production – Motivation makes workers work sincerely for completing the task assigned to them. By this, there is a possibility of utilizing the enterprise resources, viz., human, physical and financial, to the maximum.

(2) Reduced employee turnover and absenteeism – Attractive motivational schemes bring about satisfaction to employees and by this, their commitment to organization increases and they are not easily tempted by offers from competitors. This means reduced employee turnover. Further, because of their satisfaction, they will be attending to their work regularly.

(3) Increase in efficiency and output – As motivation brings about satisfaction to employees, they work wholeheartedly. Because of this, there will be an increase in their efficiency and output.

(4) Sense of belonging – A proper system of motivational schemes promotes closer identification between enterprise and workers. The workers begin to feel that the enterprise belongs to them and the interests of the enterprise are their interests and there is no difference between them. This result in better relations between management and workers.

(5) Easy availability of right personnel – Because of the proper motivational schemes, the enterprise is in a position to attract highly talented and competent persons from external sources to serve in its organization. This helps the company in increasing its efficiency.

(6) Helps in realising organizational goals – Motivated employees develop a feeling of total involvement in the task of organization and put forth their efforts wholeheartedly for the relations of organizational goals.

Important Factors of Motivation

Following are some important factors of motivation:

1. Money – Money is the traditional factor of motivation. Peter Drucker also considered money to be the most important motivator for the employees. Today also money is a powerful motivator in developing countries. "Money" as a "motivator factor" means monetary incentives offered to all categories of employees.

2. Achievement – 'To achieve something' is a natural instinct and urge in every human being. Achievement is, therefore, said to be one of the esteem needs. Naturally chances of achievement serve as motivating factor to the employees.

3. Recognition – Every human desire to get recognised for his extra ordinary performance or any great or positive thing achieved by him. This satisfies his ego. In such conditions he is automatically motivated to perform better. Getting recognition is also another need of a human being. Thus hard work, devotion outstanding performance by the employee must be recognised by the organisation.

4. Advancement – Employee's urge for self-advancement is also powerful factor of motivation. Many employees are always after their advancement may be called as self actualisation. It is the apex level of needs which always motivates the employees.

5. The work itself – Work motivating factor is a basic factor of motivation. Every human being keeps himself busy in some work and earns money for livelihood.

6. The growth – The possibility of growth gives satisfaction to the employees. If the organisation provides opportunities for personal growth of employees, they will be highly motivated.

7. Responsibility – The opportunities of higher responsibility motivate the employees more, as they get along with higher responsibility more authority also. Therefore responsibility is also motivating factor.

8. Job Security, Working condition, Status are same factors of motivation.

Techniques for Motivation :

Following are the main techniques of motivating the personnel in an organization:

1. Monetary Techniques:

These techniques are based on this popular belief that a person works for money. Hence, an attraction of getting more money will prove to be the most powerful motivator. Incentives such as more pay (through various premium plans), fringe benefits, security of tenure and condition of service are some examples of the monetary techniques of motivation.

2. Job-Based Techniques:

These techniques are based on social, human and psychological beliefs. Job simplification, job rotation, job enlargement, job enrichment, freedom in planning for work, sense of recognition, responsibility and achievement are some examples of such technique.

3. MBO Technique:

Peter Drucker, a well-known author of management, has developed this technique which emphasizes on self-control and self-motivation. It is a participatory technique of motivation whereby managers and their subordinates jointly participate in achieving the common goals. It requires an emphasis on the MBO policy in the concern.

4. Leadership Styles:

Leadership styles or supervisory techniques also have a great role in moti¬vation of employees. Autocratic, democratic, and free-rein techniques of leadership are important styles and have their own implications for employee motivation, morale and productivity. The management must try different supervisory styles in different circumstances for different employees.

5. Group-Based Techniques:

Herbert Bonner, a well-known author, has advocated group-based techniques for motivating the employees. According to him, 'Motivation is not wholly, nor even primarily, an individual variable. Certainly its force and direction are functions of the social situation in which it arises and is exercised'. Hence, management should foster group consciousness and cohesiveness among individual employees by laying down general norms and guidelines of work for the group as a whole.

6. Sensitivity Training:

This is a technique of training given to groups of managers (known as T-groups) themselves so that they behave with and motivate their subordinates better. The sensitivity training is imparted to make the managers understand themselves better, becoming more open-minded, developing insight into group process and cultivating a systematic approach towards the problem of motivation.

A manager thus trained is supposed to be more consistently able and willing to communicate with his/her subordinates and inspire them to contribute their best to the common goals and objectives.

Employee Motivation – Types:

Motivation is an organised way of inducement to the employees. The way management selects the method to inspire the workers will depend upon the understanding of management about the workers' need.

Thus, motivation can be classified as:

1. Positive motivation.
2. Negative motivation.

1. Positive Motivation:

Positive motivation is a reward-oriented method. According to Edwin B. Flippo, "Positive motivation is a process attempting to influence others to execute their will through the possibility of gain or reward." People work for incentives viz., Praise, Prestige, Promotion and Pay (Wages).

Positive motivation includes the following aspects like:

i. Praise and credit for work done,

ii. A sincere concern for the subordinates,

iii. Competition,

iv. Participation pride,

v. Delegation of authority,

vi. Appreciation, and

vii. Pay (Wages).

2. Negative Motivation:

This is intended to create fear, mainly backed by force, coercion/compulsion. This can further be of two kinds – financial and non-financial. Negative financial motivation is inflicted on an individual by making a reduction in his pay or wage, etc., and includes denial of privileges- leave, overtime, perks and so on. This is mainly based on 'force and fear'.

A person fears, for he knows the consequences of not performing the duty assigned to him. Management, at times, threatens the worker with 'Pay off, 'Demotion', etc., if he does not comply the instructions passed on with him. Negative motivation has limitations because punishment may lead to 'Hostile attitude' amongst the workers and there is every possibility of outburst of riots/strikes, etc., when this negative tool is used excessively.

Recent trend in HRM is to avoid negative motivation and integrate workers for a long-lasting relationship with the management.

Theories of Motivation

1. Hierarchy of Needs:

One of the most well-known theories of motivation is Maslow's (1954) hierarchy of needs. Maslow highlighted on primary needs as motivators as per hierarchy of needs.

The primary needs of an individual are as follows:

i. Physiological – The need to survive; for example, for food, drink, health.

ii. Safety – Physical and emotional security, such as clothing, shelter, protection against unemployment, and old age pension.

iii. Social needs/love and belonging – The desire for affection and the need to belong within the family and in society.

iv. Esteem – Accomplishment and achievement that is recognized and appreciated by someone who matters brings a sense of self-respect and bolsters self-esteem. The achiever feels good about the self.

v. Self-actualization – To utilize one's potential to the maximum, working with and for one's fellow beings.

Usually, the fulfilment of primary needs leads to higher order needs and, thereby, the primary needs related motivators become redundant for some people.

Maslow needs hierarchy theory

2. Theory X and Theory Y:

Douglas McGregor (1960) proposed two distinct views of human beings—theory X that was labelled negative, and theory Y, that was labelled positive. Under theory X, managers assume that the employee does not like work, and given a chance would avoid it. Employees need to be coerced and controlled, or punished to achieve goals; they will avoid responsibilities and basically seek formal direction.

The majority of workers like security and place it above all other factors. As against these negative assumptions about human behaviour under theory X, managers make positive assumptions under theory Y.

They believe that employees view work as something natural such as play, rest, or relaxation; people are basically self-directed and self-controlled; an average person accepts and seeks responsibility; and above all, the ability to innovate is widely distributed throughout the population and is not necessarily among those who hold managerial positions.

The major contribution by McGregor was in line with the framework given by Maslow in the hierarchy of needs. Theory X assumed dominance of lower level needs in individuals, while theory Y assumes the dominance of a higher order of needs in individuals. McGregor himself believed that theory Y is more valid and dependable than theory X.

The major application of this theory lies in managers making assumptions about the employees and turning to motivators that would work under each of the assumption.

Related Theories:

Some factors motivate while other do not. The need for job satisfaction acts as a motivator. Herzberg (1966) identified hygiene and comfort related environmental factors as leading to improvement in productivity. According to him, it is not the work but the way work is being performed that motivates people.

In his book Professional People and Manual Workers, Myers (1964), stated that people are motivated by the challenge in a job, which brings a feeling of achievement, responsibility, growth, advancement, fulfilment, enjoyment of work itself, and earned recognition. Workers become dissatisfied when opportunities for meaningful achievement are lacking or eliminated.

Herzberg had also considered that feelings of job satisfaction were more important than money for persuading people to contribute more and increase productivity. Myers, however, defined job satisfaction in more detail. Once the basic factors for job satisfaction were met by the worker, attempts were made to take the satisfaction to another level by job enlargement and job enrichment.

Job enlargement consists of making jobs more challenging and interesting by increasing carried out. Job enrichment refers to providing greater growth opportunities to the employee. Hence, motivation towards better performance depends on the satisfaction of needs for responsibility, achievement, recognition, and growth.

The intensity of these needs varies from person to person and from time to time, and so does the extent to which they are motivated. The term 'recognition' in the definition includes money rewards. Note that both job satisfaction and money are motivating factors. One works to achieve what one needs and does not have. This could be either one of the two factors or both.

In reaction to Maslow's hierarchy of needs, Alderfer propounded the theory of existence, relatedness, and growth (ERG). Alderfer's ERG theory was first published in 1969 in an article titled 'An Empirical Test of a New Theory of Human Need' in Psychological Review.

The ERG theory approaches the question of 'what motivates a person to act?' or 'why do we ever do anything?' The theory assumes that all human activity is motivated by needs. Existence (E) needs are material and physiological desires. Relatedness (R) needs are relationships with other people that are fulfilled by sharing thoughts and feelings with others. Growth (G) needs motivate people to change themselves or their environment.

These needs are realized by the complete utilization of existing capacities and developing new capacities. David McClelland (1961) proposed that each of us have three fundamental needs that exist in different proportions. These affect both how we are motivated and how we attempt to motivate others. The most important needs for a manager, according to McClelland, are the needs for achievement, affiliation, and power.

i. Need for achievement – A manager seeks achievement, this is realized by the attainment of goals and advancement, a strong need for feedback, sense of accomplishment, and progress.

ii. Need for affiliation – Need for friendship, interaction and to be liked.

iii. Need for power – Managers are motivated by authority and seek to exercise influence and to make an impact, that is, to lead and to increase personal status and prestige.

A low need for affiliation and a moderate to high need for power are associated with managerial success for both higher- and lower-level managers.

Significance of Motivation

Motivation is important in view of the following reasons:

1. Every employee has a set of unfulfilled needs. Employer, by fulfilling some of those needs, can motivate the employee thereby achieving the organization's overall objectives.

2. Motivational initiatives unearth the potential of the employees. This leads to optimum performance which in turn brings down the cost of operation. Both optimum performance and consequent lower cost paves way for achieving maximum efficiency.

3. Highly motivated employees self-direct themselves; they need no persuasion to observe safety precautions, repeated insistence on saving material, time and resources. Thus, self-discipline caused by motivation facilitates optimum utilization of productive resources.

4. There is less scope for workplace accidents, damage to tools and equipment, mishandling of machine, breakages, etc., in facilities where motivation has been applied in full force.

5. Registration of grievances and redressal thereof are out of place in organizations, putting in place different motivational tools.

6. Strike, lockout and mediation will hardly arise in organizations which have set in motion various motivational techniques.

7. There may be minimum attrition i.e., employees leaving the organization where workers are kept motivated to the hilt.

Issues in Motivation :

1. Employee Engagement:

A robust employee engagement programme figures on the top of every organization's HR agenda today. Employee engagement is the alignment of employee's goals, aspirations and values with those of the organization and achievement of goal compatibility. The various parameters of employee engagement are job satisfaction, organizational commitment, effort, proficiency, pro-activity and intention to stay.

More than one-third of the employees (42%) in India are engaged with their place of work, combining maximum job satisfaction with maximum contribution, putting India at top of a survey by global consulting firm Blessing White Inc, during summer and autumn of 2012.The percentage of employees engaged has been increased from 37% in 2011.

2. Fun at Work:

Fun at work, which is an important part of motivation, is now a corporate buzzword. Most companies are adopting unique approaches to motivate the employees through fun activities.

Tavant Technologies has instituted a wide range of initiatives to encourage and foster employee motivation at workplace which are as follows:

a. Lunching of rewards and recognition programmes named as Tavant Excellence Awards,

b. Lunching of A Spot Award Scheme and Best Interviewer Award.

c. Starting of Killing Geeks' Boredom (KGB) forum which conducts various fun activities such as Tavant Premier League (TPL), Ping Pong Wars (PPW) and online games such as KodeBrk and Pehchaan Kaun.

d. Mentoring and grooming initiatives such as discussing career paths through programmes like Career Development Initiative (CDI) and Individual Development Plan (IDP).

e. Encouraging work-life-balance and a flexible leave policy.

f. Supporting an open communication channel through open house sessions, monthly newsletter from the CEO, etc.

g. Valuing good health of employees through stress management, health camps, parenting, personal counselling, nutrition, yoga etc.

h. Covering various indoor games and outdoor sports through Synergy: the month long sporting event.

Aviva Life Insurance practices the following methods to motivate its employees:

a. Creating a Base Camp-a challenging, fun and organized series of spaces, events, and initiatives.

The Base Camp has seven peaks such as:

i. Community Climber Activities for CSR exposure.

ii. Financial Climber Activities for providing tax and legal assistance.

iii. Career Climber Activities on presentation skills, time management skills, grooming, etc.

iv. Fit Climber Activities like marathons, cricket tournaments, adventure clubs.

v. Social Climber Stage for kid's day, festival etc.

vi. Personal Climber Activities to create a fit mind through life skills workshops, personal counselling sessions.

vii. Possibility Climber Activities to create forums for expression such as "my voice portal".

b. Lunching of CEO Awards Programme

c. Lunching of IDEAs interactive channel for inviting ideas and

d. Taking Talent initiative for identifying, building and managing the strong performers.

3. Management of Office Space:

Managing office space is now days one of the important factors of motivation. Nobody wants to work in an office that is gloomy, unstructured and without any personality. An office is a place where working professionals spend a good deal of their time during the day. They see the same interiors every single day, day in and day out, so attention should be given in the way the office space is designed and maintained.

There should be a distinct characteristic that should be reflected in the office space, which gives one a sense of belonging and cheer to the employees working there. Fresh paint, integrating new or refurbished furniture, improving task or accent lighting and defining spaces with area rugs and seasonal plants are some examples of innovations in designing office space.

Office space management is a dedicated balancing act which gives a positive impact in terms of low absenteeism, reduces employee turnover, increases productivity and many more. On one hand employers want their office space to be inviting and pleasant for both employees and visitors, while on the other hand, they are also concerned about its professional look and feel.

Office space management is gaining importance in Indian organizations today as they are realizing that it is another step towards ensuring employee engagement leading to increased motivation. When the office environment is welcoming and unique, employees feel a sense of happiness when reporting to work every day.

Organizations can strive to make their office a healthy and comfortable workplace by using accessories that make the place approachable. Proper lighting and a functional design to minimize discomfort and distraction can help employees work more effectively and productively.

Employee Morale and Productivity Relation

Morale refers to someone's emotional and mental state. It can also refer to an individual's or a groups' sense of purpose and level of confidence regarding future outcomes.

When we talk about morale at work, we're referring to how your team members feel about the business, the work they do, and their place in the company.

Many research studies have been conducted across various locations, industries, and demographics to discover if there is a link between employee morale and productivity. Several studies indicate that morale can be directly tied to productivity.

Results also show that employee engagement directly impacts productivity and morale is a significant factor in an employee's level of engagement. Many of the factors that affect, such as empowering employees, building bonds with other employees and leaders, and providing rewards and recognition, also impact morale.

This link between morale and engagement means that boosting employee morale can directly and indirectly increase productivity.

Measurement of employee morale

Understanding the link between employee morale and productivity is only the first step toward improving employee and team performance. The next step is determining how to measure employee morale so that you can understand the current state of your team and track changes in morale over time.

One of the best ways to measure morale is through employee surveys. For the best results, make the surveys anonymous, have them completed routinely, and ask very specific questions that employees can answer by choosing a ranking from 1–5 or 1–10.

Some examples of survey questions are:

- Are you happy and fulfilled in your current position?
- Do you believe your hard work and effort is recognized?
- Do you feel there is room to grow in your job?
- How likely are you to stay with the company?

Another option for measuring employee morale is to conduct one-on-one interviews on a regular basis. You can also assess morale by tracking symptoms, such as:

- Changes in productivity

- Changes in tardiness or absenteeism rates
- Changes in employee turnover rates

Causes Of low employee morale

If you discover employee morale is low or seems to be decreasing, it's important you find out why. After all, if a specific problem is killing morale, any solutions that don't address that problem are unlikely to help.

Some common causes of low employee morale are:

- **Poor leadership.** While it's difficult to accept that you might be the problem, often, issues start at the top. Nearly1/3 of employees thinks their current boss is a lousy manager, and roughly half have left a job because of a bad boss.
- **Unclear expectations.** If employees aren't sure that they're doing what is expected of them, it will hurt morale. Sadly, only half of employees report that they know what's expected of them at work.
- **Lack of rewards.** Employees want to be rewarded for their work. When there are no rewards or incentives, they can feel their effort isn't being recognized, which will kill their morale.
- **Criticisms and punishments.** If employees are punished for mistakes, or even if they fear retribution for potential errors, it can ruin their confidence. Keep in mind that taking away a previous benefit, like cancelling casual Fridays, can also feel like a punishment.
- **Negative co-workers.** Unfortunately, one negative team member can quickly drag down the rest. If someone is frequently worrying or complaining, their low morale can rub off on the other employees.
- **Fear of the unknown.** As we discussed early, morale encompasses an employee's outlook of the future. If they have reason to worry that their future isn't secure, it will erode their morale. For instance, office gossip about the company losing money or potential layoffs will often damage morale.

How to improve employee morale

Removing any direct causes of low morale should help improve employee satisfaction and happiness at work. Here are some additional actions you can take to increase employee morale and productivity:

- **Touch base regularly.** Showing you care about your employee's mental state can help improve morale. Regular one-on-ones can not only help you assess morale, but they can also help your employees feel like you're interested in their well-being and development.

- **Be transparent.** Reports show that 70% of employees say they're most engaged when senior leadership continually updates and communicates company strategy. Using objectives and key results (OKRs) can help your team see the larger picture and how their work fits into it.
- **Celebrate.** Celebrating big and small accomplishments helps your team feel recognized and appreciated for their hard work. Celebrating non-work events like birthdays can also help promote team bonding and make employees happier.
- **Emphasize work-life balance.** Less time spent at work can make employees feel happier and more relaxed. It can also boost their productivity.

  Include your team in decisions. If employees don't feel that they're being considered in the decision-making process, it will make them feel undervalued and powerless.
- **Reward employees.** Teams and individuals should be rewarded for their hard work and commitment. Whether the reward is public recognition of work well done or a gift card to their favourite restaurant, regularly rewarding employees helps increase morale.
- **Encourage feedback.** Asking for honest feedback, responding positively, and addressing issues will increase your team's happiness and their faith that you're in their corner and want to help them succeed.
- **Promote team bonding.** Planning team events outside of work hours can help build a sense of belonging and unity that can, in turn, boost morale. Even remote teams can use tools like Zoom to participate in virtual team building activities.

Nature of Employee Morale:

Morale represents a composite of feelings, attitudes, and sentiments that contribute to general feelings of satisfactions. It is a state of mind and spirit affecting willingness to work, which, in turn, affects organizational and individual objectives. It describes the overall group satisfaction.

1. High morale and low morale:

If the enthusiasm and willingness to work of a group is high, we can say morale is high and vice versa. Just as good health is essential for an individual, high morale is necessary for an organization. High morale represents an attitude of satisfaction with desire to continue and willingness to strive for the goals of the group. Under conditions of high morale, workers have few grievances, frustrations, and complaints. They are clear about the goals—individual and organizational—and are satisfied with human relations in the organization.

2. Morale versus motivation:

Morale should be distinguished from motivation. Although both are cognitive concepts, they are quite different. Morale is a composite of feelings, attitudes and sentiments that contribute to general feeling of satisfaction at the workplace. But motivation is something that moves a person to action.

It is a process of stimulating individuals to action to accomplish the desired goal. It is a function of drives and needs. Motivation is concerned with 'mobilization of energy', whereas morale is concerned with 'mobilization of sentiments'.

3. Morale affects productivity:

Morale has a direct effect on productivity. High morale leads to high productivity and low morale leads to low productivity.

4. Measurement of morale:

It is hard to measure morale directly as it is an intangible state of mind of the workers.

Methods used for measuring the morale of the employee indirectly:

a. Observation:

The managers can measure the morale of the employees by keenly observing and studying their activities and behaviour. Since the manager is close to the scene of action, they can always find out unusual behaviours and report promptly. Observation is not a very reliable way of measuring morale.

b. Attitude or morale survey:

Survey helps to know the opinion of the employees either by direct interview or by questionnaires. Efforts are made to find out the view of employees about their job, co-workers, supervisors, and the organization.

c. Morale indicators:

Employee morale can be measured by examining company records regarding absenteeism, labour turnover, fluctuations in output, quality records, excessive waste and scrap, training records, accident rate, and the number of grievances filed.

d. Suggestion boxes:

Employees can be asked to put in their complaints, protests, and suggestions in suggestion boxes even without disclosing their identity. Morale generates long-term benefits such as improving the goodwill and increasing the productivity for the organization, and a satisfied employee is an asset to the organization.

Significance/Importance/Benefits of Morale:

Morale is an important part of organizational climate. It is a vital ingredient of organization success because it reflects the attitudes and sentiments of organizational members towards the organization, its objectives, and policies. Morale is the total satisfaction that employees derive from their job, their work group, their boss, their organization and their environment.

Benefits of High Morale:

Morale of employees must be kept high to achieve the following benefits:

1. Willing cooperation towards objectives of the organization.
2. Loyalty to the organization and its leadership or management
3. Good discipline—voluntary conformity to rules and regulations
4. High degrees of employees' interest in their jobs and organization
5. Pride in the organization
6. Reduction of rates of absenteeism and labour turnover
7. Happy employees are productive employees

Indicators of Low Morale:

Low morale indicates the presence of mental unrest. Such a situation will have the following adverse consequences;

1. High rates of absenteeism and labour turnover
2. Excessive complaints and grievances
3. Frustration among the workers
4. Friction among the workers and their groups
5. Antagonism towards leadership of the organization
6. Lack of discipline

Measures to Improve Morale:

Morale building is a continuous process which cannot be stopped even for a moment. Morale cannot be maintained at a high level forever. It is dynamic. Morale building may be done either on individual basis or on ground basis. Morale building on group basis is always preferable. Group morale can be increased by understanding the group dynamics. It will automatically achieve the individual morale.

Following are the important steps to achieve high morale among employees:

1. Fair remuneration:

Remuneration should be fair and equitable since this is the most important factor affecting the employee morale. The basic and incentive pay plans should be fair.

2. Incentives:

Monetary and non-monetary incentives to the employees are important to motivate them. Employees can be offered extra perks to improve morale. These can include time off, the option to work from home, a flexible schedule, or simple recognition when work is well done.

3. Work environment:

The condition of work should be friendly for the employee's mental and physical well-being. Employees may be more concerned with intangible benefits, such as work- life balance and the atmosphere in the workplace.

4. Job satisfaction:

Well-placed employees take pride and interest in their work and feel satisfied.

5. Two-way communication:

Two-way communication (upward and downward) is necessary to know the sentiments of employees in the organization. Organization policies and programmes should be properly communicated to employees.

6. Training:

In this ever-evolving world of new technologies and ideas, employees need to stay up- to-date with developments in their field. Training gives psychological satisfaction to employees and improves their performance.

7. Worker's participation:

Workers must be consulted and taken into confidence whenever a change is to be introduced.

8. Social group activities:

These activities encourage employees to take on a community-service project together. Employees will likely enjoy the opportunity to give back to their local com¬munity. Management should encourage social group activities by the workers. This will help to develop greater group cohesiveness for building high morale.

9. Counselling:

Employee counselling helps the employees with their problems and complaints, and provides an opportunity to get back on track since the counsellor is impartial. It helps to reduce absenteeism and labour turnover. The release of emotional tension alone may serve to minimize dissatisfactions.

10. Treating employees with respect:

Treat employees with the courtesy and respect they deserve— say please and thank you. Ask about their weekend, and take an interest in projects that they are working on. Thus, an unhappy employee is an unproductive employee.

A company needs to pursue policies like the ones mentioned above to help its business become a more enjoyable place to work. Not only will employees start to look forward to their workdays, the organization will benefit from the new-found efficiency.

Productivity

The concept of productivity can be applicable to any economy, small, medium and large business, government and individuals. Productivity aims at the maximum utilization of resources for yielding as many goods and services as possible, desired by consumers at lowest possible cost. Productivity is the ratio of output in a period of time to the input in the same period time.

Productivity can measured with the help of following formula:

$$\text{Productivity} = \frac{\text{Output in a Period of Time}}{\text{Input in the Same Period of Time}}$$

Productivity Measurement Equation

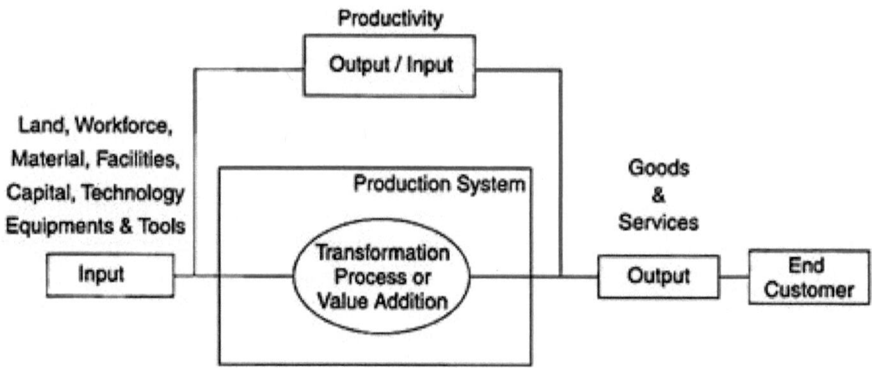

System Concept of Productivity

In simple terms Productivity is the ratio of output to some or all of the resources used to produce the output. Productivity can thus be measured as:

$$\text{Productivity} = \frac{\text{Quantity of Goods and Services Produced}}{\text{Ammount of Resource Used}}$$

Mathematically $$P = \frac{O}{I}$$

Productivity Equation

"Productivity is the quantitative relation between; what a firm produces and what a firm uses as a resource to produce output, i.e. arithmetic ratio of amount produced (output) to the amount of resources (input)".

"Productivity is an aggregate measure of the efficiency of production; it is the ratio of output to inputs i.e. capital, labor, land, energy and materials".

"Productivity refers to the efficiency of the production system and an indicator to; how well the factors of production (land, capital, labor and energy) are utilized".

Productivity is the ratio between output of wealth and input of resources used in production processes. Output means the quantity of products produced and the inputs are the various resources used in the production. The resources used may be land, building, equipment, machinery, materials, labour etc.

Productivity can be increased by the following ways:

1. Increasing the output using the same input.
2. Reducing the input by maintaining the output as constant.
3. Increasing the output to a maximum extent with a smaller increase in input.

Factors Affecting Productivity

Productivity is the outcome of several factors. These factors are so interrelated that it is difficult to identify the effect of any one factor on productivity.

1. Human:

Human nature and human behavior are the most significant determinants of productivity.

Human factors may further be classified into two categories as given below:

(a) Ability to work – Productivity of an organization depends upon the competence and calibre of its people—both workers and managers. Ability to work is governed by education, training, experience, aptitude, etc. of the employees.

(b) Willingness to work – Motivation and morale of people is the second important group of human factors that determine productivity. Wage incentive schemes, labour participation in management, communication system, informal group relations, promotion policy, union management relations, quality of leadership, etc., are the main factors governing employees' willingness to work. Working conditions like working hours, sanitation, ventilation, schools, clubs, libraries, subsidized canteen, company transport, etc., also influence the motivation and morale of employees.

2. Technological:

Technological factors exercise significant influence on the level of productivity.

The main technological factors are as follows:

(a) Size and capacity of plant

(b) Product design and standardization
(c) Timely supply of materials and fuel
(d) Rationalization and automation measures
(e) Repairs and maintenance
(f) Production planning and control
(g) Plant layout and location
(h) Materials handling system
(i) Inspection and quality control
(j) Machinery and equipment used
(k) Research and development
(l) Inventory control
(m) Reduction and utilization of waste and scrap, etc.

3. Managerial:

The competence and attitudes of managers have an important bearing on productivity. In many organizations, productivity is low despite latest technology and trained manpower. This is due to inefficient and indifferent management. Competent and dedicated managers can obtain extraordinary results from ordinary people.

Job performance of employees depends on their ability and willingness to work. Management is the catalyst to create both. Advanced technology requires knowledge workers who in turn work productively under professionally qualified managers. No ideology can win a greater output with less effort. It is only through sound management that optimum utilization of human and technical resources can be secured.

4. Natural:

Natural factors such as physical, geological, geographical and climatic conditions exert considerable influence on productivity, particularly in extractive industries. For example, productivity of labour in extreme climates (too cold or too hot) tends to be comparatively low. Natural resources like water, fuel and minerals influence productivity.

5. Sociological:

Social customs, traditions and institutions influence attitudes towards work and job. For instance, bias on the basis of caste, religion, etc., inhibited the growth of modern industry in some countries. The joint family system affected incentive to work hard in India. Close ties with land and native place hampered stability and discipline among industrial labour.

6. Political:

Law and order, stability of Government, harmony between States, etc. are essential for high productivity in industries. Taxation policies of the Government influence willingness to work, capital formation, modernization and expansion of plants, etc. Industrial policy affects the size, and capacity of plants. Tariff policies influence competition. Elimination of sick and inefficient units helps to improve productivity.

7. Economic:

Sizes of the market, banking and credit facilities, transport and communication systems, etc. are important factors influencing productivity.

Productivity is an economics term which refers to the ratio of product to what is required to produce the product. Productivity is outcome of several interrelated factors. All the factors which are related to input and output components of a production process are likely to affect productivity.

So, there are many factors which can influence productivity; such as internal and external. Knowing the internal and external factors that affect productivity of an Industrial organization; give industrial engineers; the intelligence, they needs to sort out the low performance of resources and make strategic plans for the future.

The best thing about internal factors is that you can control many of them. External factors are all those things that are beyond your control. To deal with all these factors we need different people and variety of techniques and methods.

Some of the Other Factors

The factors influencing productivity can be classified broadly into two categories:

(A) Controllable Factors.

(B) Uncontrollable Factor.

(A) Controllable Factors:

Controllable Factors are considered as internal factors. These are the factors which are in control of industrial organization.

Controllable factors are:

1. Material and Power:

Improved quality of raw materials and increased use of power have a favorable effect on productivity. An effort to reduce materials and energy consumption brings about considerable improvement in productivity.

It consists of:

i. Selection of quality material and right material.

ii. Control of wastage and scrap.

iii. Effective stock control.

iv. Development of sources of supply.

v. Optimum energy utilization and energy savings.

2. Machinery and Plant Layout:

The size of the plant and the capacity utilization has direct bearing on productivity. Production below or above the optimum level will be uneconomical and will tend towards lower level of productivity. The arrangement of machines and position in the plant and the setup of the wore-bench of an individual worked will determine how economically and efficiently production will be ferried out.

3. Human Factors:

Human nature and human behavior are the most significant determinants of productivity. Human factors include both their ability as well as their willingness.

i. Ability to Work:

Ability to work is governed by education, training, experience and aptitude of the employees. Productivity of an organization depends upon the competence and caliber of its people (both workers and managers).

ii. Willingness to Work:

Motivation and morale of people are very important factors that determine productivity. These are affected by wage incentive schemes, labour participation in management, communication systems, informal group relations, promotion policy, union Management relations, quality of leadership, working hours, sanitation, ventilation, subsidized canteen and company transport etc.

4. Organization and Managerial Factors:

Organization factor include various steps taken by the organization towards maintaining better industrial relations such as delegation and decentralization of authority. These factors also influence motivation likewise the existence of group, with higher productivity as their goal is likely to contribute to the organization objectives.

The competence and attitudes of managers have an important bearing on productivity. Competent and dedicated managers can obtain extraordinary results from ordinary people. Job performance of employees depends on their ability and willingness to work.

5. Technological Factors:

Technological factors exert significant influence on the level of productivity.

These include the following:

i. Size and capacity of plant

ii. Product design and standardization

iii. Production planning and control

iv. Plant layout and location

v. Materials handling system

vi. Inspection and quality control

vii. Machinery and equipment used

viii. Research and development

(B) Uncontrollable Factors:

Uncontrollable factors are known as external factors and these factors are beyond the control of the individual industrial organization.

Uncontrollable factors are:

1. Economic Political and Social Changes:

There are economic, social and political factor that affects the productivity.

i. Economic Factors like Size of the market, banking and credit facilities, transport and communication systems, etc. is important factors influencing productivity.

ii. Political Factors like Law and order, stability of government, harmony between states etc. are essential for high productivity in industries Taxation policies of the government influence willingness to work, capital formation, modernization and expansion of plants etc. Industrial policy affects the size, and capacity of plants. Elimination of sick and inefficient units also helps to improve productivity.

iii. Social Factors like Social customs, traditions and institutions influence attitudes towards work and job. For instance, bias on the basis of caste, religion, etc., inhibited the growth of modern industry in some countries. The joint family system affected incentive to work hard in India. Close ties with land and native place hampered stability and discipline among industrial labour.

2. Natural Resources:

Natural factors such as physical, geographical and climate conditions exert considerable influence on productivity, particularly in extreme climates (too cold or too hot) tends to be comparatively low. Natural resources like water, fuel and minerals influence productivity.

3. Government Factor:

Government policies and programs are significant to productivity practices of government agencies, transport and communication power, and fiscal policies (interest rates, taxes) influence productivity to the greater extent.

Importance of Productivity

Productivity has become almost synonymous for progress. The resources of a country are generally limited. Therefore, higher productivity is essential for improving living standards and for the prosperity of a nation. Higher productivity requires elimination of waste in all forms. Higher productivity leads to economic growth and social progress.

It is only by improving productivity that employees can get better wages and working conditions and more employment opportunities. Higher productivity brings lower prices for consumers and higher dividend for shareholders. It improves the exports and foreign exchange reserves of a country. Thus, productivity is the key to prosperity.

Higher productivity is of special significance in an underdeveloped country like India. Mass poverty and unemployment cannot be eliminated without increasing productivity in agriculture, industry and all other areas of human activity. According to John W. Kendrick, "the chief means where by human kind can raise itself out of poverty to a condition of relative material influence is by increasing productivity".

In brief, higher productivity provides the following importance:

(i) It helps to reduce the cost of production per unit through more economical or efficient use of resources.

(ii) Reduction in costs helps to improve the profits of a business. The enterprise can more successfully compete in the market.

(iii) The gains of higher productivity can be passed on to consumers in the form of lower prices and/or better quality of products.

(iv) Similarly, gains of higher productivity can be shared with workers in the form of higher wages or salaries and better working conditions.

(v) Availability of quality goods at reasonably low prices helps to improve the standard of living in the country.

(vi) Due to higher productivity, a firm can survive and grow better. This helps to generate more employment opportunities.

(vii) A more productive enterprise can better export goods and earn valuable foreign exchange for the country.

(viii) Higher productivity means better utilization of the country's resources, which helps to control inflation in the country.

Ways to Improve Productivity and Quality of Products

It is vital to develop a high rate of productivity because it is the foundation of the business's future growth.

There are many ways by which productivity can be increased:

i. Adoption of up to date technology in machines and equipment.

ii. Implementing a proper system of managerial planning and control.

iii. Effective time management.

iv. Maintenance of work facilities in factories.

v. Standardization and automation for mass production.

vi. Empower employees by providing training and an environment conducive for personal is well as organizational growth.

vii. Let workers participate in management.

viii. Provide a flexible work schedule instead of rigid working hours.

ix. Clear communication should be there between management and workers.

Way 1. Combining the Resources for Production:

Managers attempt to utilize the resources just described in a manner that achieves production at a low cost. They combine the various resources with the use of work stations and assembly lines. A work station is an area in which one or more employees are assigned a specific task. A work station may require machinery and equipment as well as employees.

An assembly line consists of a sequence of work stations in which each work station is designed to cover specific phases of the production process. The production of a single product may require several work stations, with each station using employees, machinery, and materials.

Since the cost of all these resources along with the building can be substantial, efficient management of the production process can reduce expenses, which can convert into higher profits.

Employees use buildings, machinery, and equipment to convert materials into a product or service. For example, employees of printing firms use machines for typesetting, printing, and binding to produce books. Employees of General Nutrition Centers (GNC) use its manufacturing plant (which is the size of four football fields) to produce more than 150,000 bottles of vitamins per day.

Way 2. Selecting a Site:

A critical decision in production management is the selection of a site (location) for the factory or office. Location can significantly affect the cost of production and therefore the firm's ability to compete against other firms. This is especially true for industrial firms such as Bethlehem Steel and DaimlerChrysler, which require a large investment in plant and equipment.

Factors Affecting the Site Decision:

Several factors must be considered when determining the optimal site.

The most relevant factors are identified below:

i. Cost of Workplace Space:

The cost of purchasing or renting workplace space (such as buildings or offices) can vary significantly among locations. Costs are likely to be high near the center of any business district where land costs are high.

Costs also tend to be higher in certain regions. For example, office rental rates are generally higher in the northeastern states than in other areas. This is one major reason why companies located in northern cities have relocated to the South during the last 10 years.

ii. Cost of Labor:

The cost of hiring employees varies significantly among locations. Salaries within a city tend to be higher than salaries outside the city for a given occupation. Salaries are also generally higher in the North than the South for a given occupation. This is another reason why many companies have relocated to the South.

iii. Tax Incentives:

Some local governments may be willing to grant tax credits to attract companies to their area. The governments offer this incentive to increase the employment level and improve economic conditions in the area.

iv. Source of Demand:

If a firm plans to sell its product in a specific location, it may establish its plant there. The costs of transporting and servicing the product can be minimized by producing at a site near the source of demand.

v. Access to Transportation:

When companies sell products across the nation, they may choose a site near their main source of transportation. They also need to be accessible so that materials can be delivered to them. Some factories and offices are established near interstate highways, rivers, or airports for this reason.

vi. Supply of Labor:

Firms that plan to hire specialized workers must be able to attract the labor needed. They may choose a location where a large supply of workers with that particular specialization exists. For instance, high-tech companies tend to locate near universities where there is an abundance of educated labor.

Way 3. Selecting the Design and Layout:

Once a site for a manufacturing plant or office is chosen, the design and layout must be determined. The design indicates the size and structure of the plant or office. The layout is the arrangement of the machinery and equipment within the factory or office.

The design and layout decisions directly affect operating expenses because they determine the costs of rent, machinery, and equipment. They may even affect the firm's interest expenses because they influence the amount of money that must be borrowed to purchase property or machinery.

Way 4. Production Control:

Once the plant and design have been selected, the firm can engage in production control, which involves the following:

(i) Purchasing materials
(ii) Inventory control
(iii) Routing
(iv) Scheduling
(v) Quality Control

(i) Purchasing Materials:

Managers perform the following tasks when purchasing supplies. First, they must select a supplier. Second, they attempt to obtain volume discounts. Third, they determine whether to delegate some production tasks to suppliers.

(ii) Inventory Control:

Inventory control is the process of managing inventory at a level that minimizes costs. It requires the management of materials inventories, work-in-process inventories, and finished goods inventories.

(iii) Routing:

Routing is the sequence (or route) of tasks necessary to complete the production of a product. Raw materials are commonly sent to various work stations so that they can be used as specified in the production process. A specific part of the production process is completed at each work station.

For example, the production of a bicycle may require (1) using materials to produce a bike frame at one work station, (2) assembling wheels at a second work station, and (3) packaging the frames and wheels that have been assembled at a third work station.

The routing process is periodically evaluated to determine whether it can be improved to allow a faster or less expensive production process. General Motors, DaimlerChrysler, and United Parcel Service have streamlined their routing process to improve production efficiency.

(iv) Scheduling:

Scheduling is the act of setting time periods for each task in the production process. A production schedule is a plan for the timing and volume of production tasks. For example, the production schedule for a bicycle may set a time of two hours for each frame to be assembled and one hour for each wheel to be assembled.

Scheduling is useful because it establishes the expected amount of production that should be achieved at each work station over a given day or week. Therefore, each employee understands what is expected.

Furthermore, scheduling allows managers to forecast how much will be produced by the end of the day, week, or month. If a firm does not meet its production schedule, it will not be able to accommodate customer orders in a timely fashion and will lose some of its customers.

(v) Quality Control:

Quality can be defined as the degree to which a product or service satisfies a customer's requirements or expectations Quality relates to customer satisfaction, which can have an effect on future sales and therefore on the future performance of the firm. Customers are more likely to purchase additional products from the same firm if they are satisfied with the quality.

Firms now realize that it is easier to retain existing customers than it is to attract new customers who are unfamiliar with their products or services. Thus, firms are increasingly recognizing the impact that the quality of their products or services can have on their overall performance.

Quality control is a process of determining whether the quality of a product or a service meets the desired quality level and identifying improvements (if any) that need to be made in the production process. Quality can be measured by assessing the various characteristics (such as how long the product lasts) that enhance customer satisfaction.

The quality of a computer may be defined by how well it works and how long it lasts. Quality may also be measured by how easy the computer is to use or by how quickly the manufacturer repairs a computer that experiences problems. All of these characteristics can affect customer satisfaction and therefore should be considered as indicators of quality.

The quality of services sold to customers must also be assessed. For example, Amazon(dot)com produces a service of fulfilling orders of books, CDs, and other products ordered over the Internet by customers. Its customers assess the quality of the service in terms of the ease with which they can send an order over the Internet whether they receive the proper order, and how quickly the products are delivered.

The act of monitoring and improving the quality of products and services produced is commonly referred to as total quality management (TQM), which was developed by W. Edwards Deming.

Among TQM's key guidelines for improving quality are the following- (1) provide managers and other employees with the education and training they need to excel in their jobs, (2) encourage employees to take responsibility and to provide leadership, and (3) encourage all employees to search for ways to improve the production process.

Production quotas are discouraged so that employees can allocate more of their time to leadership and the improvement of the production process. Many firms use teams of employees to assess quality and offer suggestions for continuous improvement.

To ensure that quality is maintained, firms periodically evaluate the methods used to measure product or service quality.

Performance Appraisal

Performance Appraisal is the systematic evaluation of the performance of employees and to understand the abilities of a person for further growth and development. Performance appraisal is generally done in systematic ways which are as follows:

- The supervisors measure the pay of employees and compare it with targets and plans.
- The supervisor analyses the factors behind work performances of employees.
- The employers are in position to guide the employees for a better performance.

Objectives of Performance Appraisal

Performance Appraisal can be done with following objectives in mind:

- To maintain records in order to determine compensation packages, wage structure, salaries raises, etc.
- To identify the strengths and weaknesses of employees to place right men on right job.
- To maintain and assess the potential present in a person for further growth and development.

- To provide a feedback to employees regarding their performance and related status.
- To provide a feedback to employees regarding their performance and related status.
- It serves as a basis for influencing working habits of the employees.
- To review and retain the promotional and other training programmes.

Advantages of Performance Appraisal

It is said that performance appraisal is an investment for the company which can be justified by following advantages:

1. Promotion:

Performance Appraisal helps the supervisors to chalk out the promotion programs for efficient employees. In this regards, inefficient workers can be dismissed or demoted in case.

2. Compensation:

Performance Appraisal helps in chalking out compensation packages for employees. Merit rating is possible through performance appraisal. Performance Appraisal trics to give worth to a performance. Compensation packages which include bonus, high salary rates, extra benefits, allowances and pre-requisites are dependent on performance appraisal. The criteria should be merit rather than seniority.

3. Employees Development:

The systematic procedure of performance appraisal helps the supervisors to frame training policies and programs. It helps to analyze strengths and weaknesses of employees so that new jobs can be designed for efficient employees. It also helps in framing future development programs.

4. Selection Validation:

Performance Appraisal helps the supervisors to understand the validity and importance of the selection procedure. The supervisors come to know the validity and thereby the strengths and weaknesses of selection procedure. Future changes in selection methods can be made in this regard.

5. Communication:

For an organization, effective communication between employees and employers is very important. Through performance appraisal, communication can be sought for in the following ways:

- Through performance appraisal, the employers can understand and accept skills of subordinates.
- The subordinates can also understand and create a trust and confidence in superiors.
- It also helps in maintaining cordial and congenial labour management relationship.
- It develops the spirit of work and boosts the morale of employees.

All the above factors ensure effective communication.

6. Motivation:

Performance appraisal serves as a motivation tool. Through evaluating performance of employees, a person's efficiency can be determined if the targets are achieved. This very well motivates a person for better job and helps him to improve his performance in the future.

Employee Performance Appraisal

The employee performance appraisal process is crucial for organizations to boost employee productivity and improve their outcomes. Performance appraisals are an annual process where an employee's performance and productivity is evaluated against a predetermined set of objectives.

Performance management is super important, not only because it is the determining factor in an employee's wage rise and promotion but also because it can evaluate an employee's skills, strengths, and shortcomings accurately.

However, the performance appraisal is rarely put to good use since existing performance appraisal methods fail to internalize employee performance results. To prevent performance appraisals from becoming nothing more than empty buzzwords, HR managers need to revamp their existing process and try implementing one of the six modern performance appraisal methods that are listed below.

Six modern performance appraisal methods

With the right performance appraisal method, organizations can enhance employee performance within the organization. A good employee performance review method can make the whole experience effective and rewarding.

1. Management by Objectives (MBO)

Management by objectives (MBO) is the appraisal method where managers and employees together identify, plan, organize, and communicate objectives to focus on during a specific appraisal period. After setting clear goals, managers and subordinates periodically discuss the progress made to control and debate on the feasibility of achieving those set objectives.

This performance appraisal method is used to match the overarching organizational goals with objectives of employees effectively while validating objectives using the SMART method to see if the set objective is specific, measurable, achievable, realistic, and time-sensitive.

At the end of the review period (quarterly, half-yearly, or annual), employees are judged by their results. Success is rewarded with promotion and a salary hike whereas failure is dealt with transfer or further training. This process usually lays more stress on tangible goals and intangible aspects like interpersonal skills, commitment, etc. are often brushed under the rug.

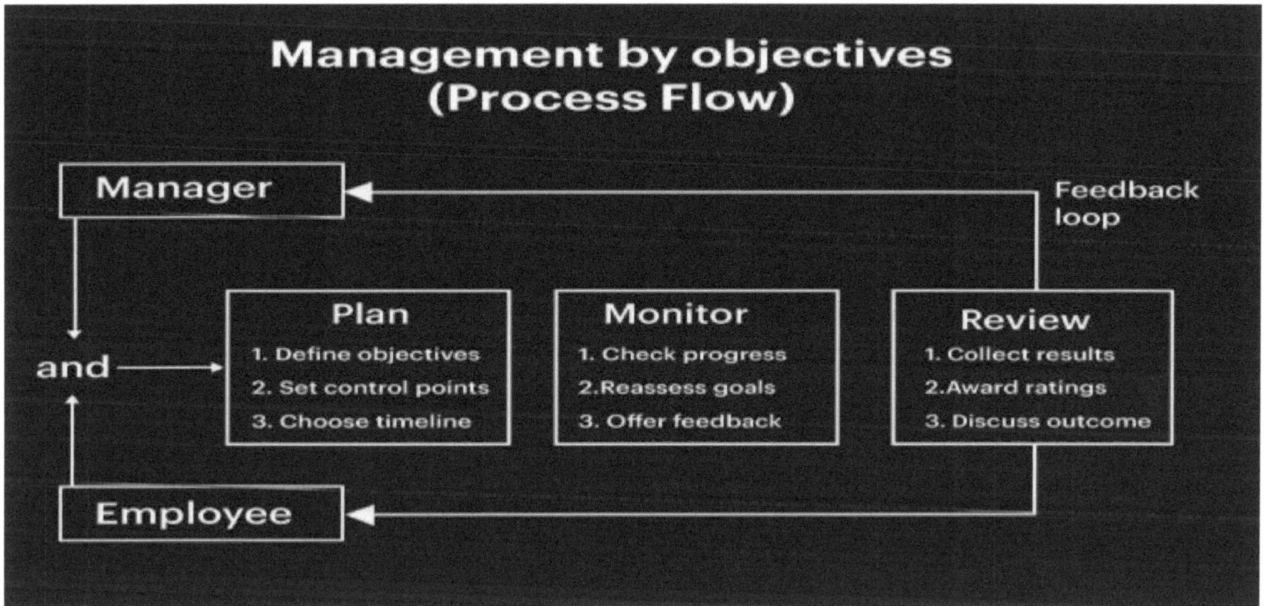

Process Flow of MBO

Incorporating MBO into your performance management process

To ensure success, the MBO process needs to be embedded in the organizational-wide goal setting and appraisal process. By incorporating MBO into the performance management process, businesses can improve employee's commitment, amplify chances for goal accomplishment, and enable employees to think futuristically.

Ideal for:

Measuring the quantitative and qualitative output of senior management like managers, directors, and executive (business of any size)

Common reason for failure:

Incomplete MBO program, inadequate corporate objectives, lack of top management involvement

Steps to implement a successful MBO program:

1. Every manager must have 5-10 goals expressed in specific, measurable terms
2. Manager can propose their goals in writing, which will be finalized after review
3. Each goal needs to include a description and a clear plan (list of tasks) to accomplish it
4. Determine how progress will be measured and how frequently (minimum quarterly)

5. List down corrective actions that will be taken if progress is not in accordance with plans
6. Ensure that goals at each level are related to the organizational objectives and levels above/below

Retail giant Walmart, uses an extensive MBO participatory approach to manage the performance of its top, middle, and first-line managers.

2. 360-Degree Feedback

360-degree feedback is a multidimensional performance appraisal method that evaluates an employee using feedback collected from the employee's circle of influence namely managers, peers, customers, and direct reports. This method will not only eliminate bias in performance reviews but also offer a clear understanding of an individual's competence.

This appraisal method has five integral components like:

1. Self-appraisals

Self-appraisals offer employees a chance to look back at their performance and understand their strengths and weaknesses. However, if self-appraisals are performed without structured forms or formal procedures, it can become lenient, fickle, and biased.

2. Managerial reviews

Performance reviews done by managers are a part of the traditional and basic form of appraisals. These reviews must include individual employee ratings awarded by supervisors as well as the evaluation of a team or program done by senior managers.

3. Peer reviews

As hierarchies move out of the organizational picture, coworkers get a unique perspective on the employee's performance making them the most relevant evaluator. These reviews help determine an employee's ability to work well with the team, take up initiatives, and be a reliable contributor. However, friendship or animosity between peers may end up distorting the final evaluation results.

4. Subordinates Appraising manager (SAM)

This upward appraisal component of the 360-degree feedback is a delicate and significant step. Reportees tend to have the most unique perspective from a managerial point of view. However, reluctance or fear of retribution can skew appraisal results.

5. Customer or client reviews

The client component of this phase can include either internal customers such as users of product within the organization or external customers who are not a part of the company but interact with this specific employee on a regular basis.

Customer reviews can evaluate the output of an employee better, however, these external users often do not see the impact of processes or policies on an employee's output.

Advantages of using 360-degree feedback:

- Increase the individual's awareness of how they perform and the impact it has on other stakeholders
- Serve as a key to initiate coaching, counselling, and career development activities
- Encourage employees to invest in self-development and embrace change management
- Integrate performance feedback with work culture and promote engagement

Ideal for:

Private sector organizations than public sector organisations as peer reviews at public sector organizations are more lenient.

Common reason for failure:

Leniency in review, cultural differences, competitiveness, ineffective planning, and misguided feedback

Top private organizations like RBS, Sainsbury's, and G4S are using 360-degree, multi-rater performance feedback to measure employee performance.

3. Assessment Centre Method

The concept of assessment centre was introduced way back in 1930 by the German Army but it has been polished and tailored to fit today's environment. The assessment centre method enables employees to get a clear picture of how others observe them and the impact it has on their performance. The main advantage of this method is that it will not only assess the existing performance of an individual but also predict future job performance.

During the assessment, employees are asked to take part in social-simulation exercises like in-basket exercises, informal discussions, fact-finding exercises, decision-making problems, role-play, and other exercises that ensure success in a role. The major drawback of this approach is that it is a time and cost intensive process that is difficult to manage.

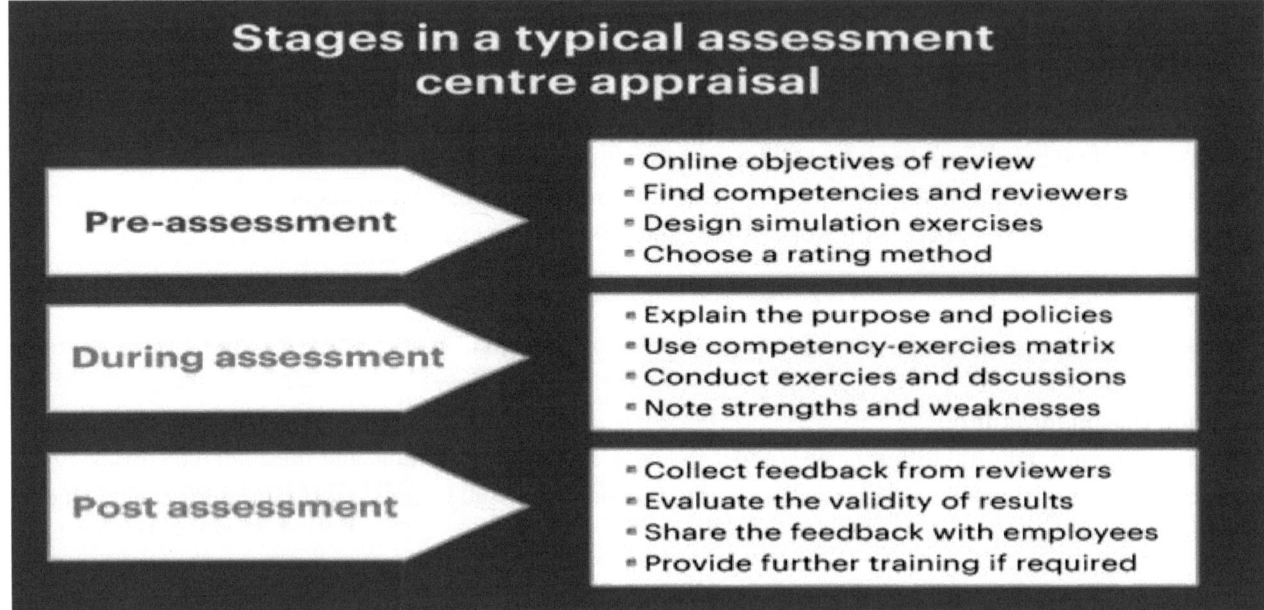

Stages in Centre Appraisal

Advantages of the assessment centre method:

- Enhance a participant's knowledge, boost his/her thought process, and improve employee efficiency
- Can be tailored to fit different roles, competencies, and business needs
- Offer an insight of the employee's personality (ethics, tolerance, problem-solving skill, introversion/extroversion, adaptability, etc.)

Ideal for:

Manufacturing organizations, service-based companies, educational institutions, and consulting firms to identify future organizational leaders and managers.

Guidelines to implement assessment centre practice:

1. Use job analysis to determine the components of effective performance
2. Identify performance metrics that can be measured using this assessment centre

3. Classify meaningful and relevant candidate behaviour in the assessment process
4. Find assessment techniques that can ideally elicit ideal behavioural information
5. Spot assessors and assessee's excluding immediate supervisors
6. Provide thorough training to assessors and reviewers
7. Maintain a system of performance records for each candidate
8. Review records and reward employee or provide training accordingly

Microsoft, Philips, and several other organizations use the assessment centre practice to identify future leaders in their workforce.

4. Behaviourally Anchored Rating Scale (BARS)

Behaviorally anchored rating scales (BARS) bring out both the qualitative and quantitative benefits in a performance appraisal process. BARS compare employee performance with specific behavioral examples that are anchored to numerical ratings.

Each performance level on a BAR scale is anchored by multiple BARS statements which describe common behaviors that an employee routinely exhibits. These statements act as a yardstick to measure an individual's performance against predetermined standards that are applicable to their role and job level.

The first step in BARS creation is generation of critical incidents that depict typical workplace behavior. The next step is editing these critical incidents into a common format and removing any redundancy. After normalization, the critical instances are randomized and assessed for effectiveness. Remaining critical incidents are used to create BARS and evaluate employee performance.

Advantages of using BARS:

- Enjoy clear standards, improved feedback, accurate performance analysis, and consistent evaluation
- Eliminate construct-irrelevant variance in performance appraisal ratings by emphasis more on specific, concrete, and observable behaviors
- Decrease any chance for bias and ensure fairness throughout the appraisal process

Ideal for:

Businesses of all sizes and industries can use BARS to assess the performance of their entire workforce from the entry level agent to c-suite executives

Common drawbacks of BARS:

1. High chance for subjectivity in evaluations

2. Hard to make compensation and promotion decisions
3. Time-consuming to create and implement
4. Demands more from managers and senior executives

5. Psychological Appraisals

Psychological appraisals come in handy to determine the hidden potential of employees. This method focuses on analyzing an employee's future performance rather than their past work. These appraisals are used to analyze seven major components of an employee's performance such as interpersonal skills, cognitive abilities, intellectual traits, leadership skills, personality traits, emotional quotient, and other related skills.

Qualified psychologists conduct a variety of tests (in-depth interviews, psychological tests, discussions, and more) to assess an employee effectively. However, it is a rather slow and complex process and the quality of results is highly dependent on the psychologist who administers the procedure.

Specific scenarios are taken into account while performing psychological appraisal. For instance, the way in which an employee deals with an aggressive customer can be used to appraise his/her persuasion skills, behavioral response, emotional response, and more.

Advantages of psychological appraisals:

1. Extract measurable, objective data about not just an employee's performance but also potential
2. Can be deployed easily when compared with other performance appraisal methods
3. Offer introverted or shy employees a platform to shine and prove their potential

Ideal for:

Large enterprises can use psychological appraisals for an array of reasons including development of leadership pipeline, team building, conflict resolutions, and more.

Common reasons for failure:

Absence of proper training, lack of trained professionals to administer reviews, and nervousness or anxiety of candidates can skew results.

Ford motors, Exxon Mobil, Procter & Gamble use psychological appraisals to test the personality and performance of their employees.

6. Human-Resource (Cost) Accounting Method

Human resource (cost) accounting method analyses an employee's performance through the monetary benefits he/she yields to the company. It is obtained by comparing the cost of retaining an employee (cost to company) and the monetary benefits (contributions) an organization has ascertained from that specific employee.

When an employee's performance is evaluated based on cost accounting methods, factors like unit-wise average service value, quality, overhead cost, interpersonal relationships, and more are taken into account. Its high-dependency on the cost and benefit analysis and the memory power of the reviewer is the drawback of human resources accounting method.

Advantages of the human cost accounting method:

- Effectively measure the cost and value that an employee brings to the organization
- Help identify the financial implications that an employee's performance has on the organization's bottom line

Ideal for:

Startups and small businesses where the performance of one employee can make or break the organization's success.

Implementation of human resource cost accounting method:

1. Identify the gap between the market and the current package of an employee
2. Determine the monetary and non-monetary value that an employee brings to the table
3. List down the things that an employee achieved in the review period (increase in the subscriber count, improvement in revenue, number of new deals won, etc.,)

CHAPTER FIVE

Leadership

Leadership is the ability of an individual or a group of individuals to influence and guide followers or other members of an organization.

Leadership involves making sound -- and sometimes difficult -- decisions, creating and articulating a clear vision, establishing achievable goals and providing followers with the knowledge and tools necessary to achieve those goals.

Leaders are found and required in most aspects of society, from business to politics to region to community-based organizations.

An effective leader possess the following characteristics: self-confidence, strong communication and management skills, creative and innovative thinking, perseverance in the face of failure, willingness to take risks, openness to change, and levelheadedness and reactiveness in times of crisis.

In business, individuals who exhibit these leadership qualities can ascend to executive management or C-level positions, such as CEO, CIO or president. Noteworthy individuals who have exhibited strong leadership in the technology industry include Apple founder Steve Jobs, Microsoft founder Bill Gates and Amazon CEO Jeff Bezos.

There are 7 primary leadership styles and each has its place in a leader's toolkit. Depending on the situation, wise leaders know how and when to flex from one style to another.

On a continuum, leadership styles range from autocratic at one end, to laissez-faire at the other, with a variety of styles in between.

Hopefully this list will help you differentiate between the different styles and know when to apply them. Which style is your default? And which do you need to practice?

The seven primary leadership styles are:

(1) Autocratic,

(2) Authoritative,

(3) Pace-Setting,

(4) Democratic,

(5) Coaching,

(6) Affiliative,

(7) Laissez-faire.

1. Autocratic Style

"Do as I say"

Generally, an autocratic leader believes that he or she knows more than others. They make all the decisions with little input from team members.

This command-and-control approach is typical of the past and doesn't hold much water with today's talent.

The style may still be appropriate in certain situations. For example, you can dip into an autocratic leadership style when crucial decisions need to be made on the spot, and you have the most knowledge about the situation. It also works when you're dealing with inexperienced and new team members and there's no time to wait for team members to gain familiarity with their role.

2. Authoritative Style

"Visionary" - "Follow Me"

The authoritative leadership style is the mark of confident leaders who map the way and set expectations, while engaging and energizing followers along the way.

In a climate of uncertainty, these leaders lift the fog for people. They help them see where the company is going and what's going to happen when they get there.

Unlike autocratic leaders, authoritative leaders take the time to explain their thinking: They don't just issue orders. Most of all, they allow people's input on how to achieve common goals.

3. Pace-Setting Style

"Do as I do!"

This style describes a very driven leader who sets the pace as in racing. Pacesetters set the bar high and push their team members to run hard and fast to the finish line.

While this style is effective in getting things done and driving for results, it's a style that can hurt team members. Even the most driven employees may become stressed working under this style of leadership in the long run.

This style may still serve you well if for example you're an energetic entrepreneur working with a like-minded team on developing and announcing a new product or service. This is a short term style. A pace-setting leader needs to let the air out of the tires once in a while to avoid causing team burnout.

4. Democratic Style

"What do you think?"

Democratic leaders share information with employees about anything that affects their work responsibilities and also seek employees' opinions before approving a final decision.

There are numerous benefits to this participative leadership style. It can engender trust and promote team spirit and cooperation from employees. It allows for creativity and helps employees grow and develop. A democratic leadership style gets people to do what you want to be done but in a way that *they want* to do it.

5. Coaching Style

"Consider this"

A leader who coaches views people as a reservoir of talent to be developed. A coach approach seeks to unlock people's potential.

Leaders who use a coaching style open their hearts and doors for people. They believe that everyone has power within themselves. A coaching leader gives people a little direction to help them tap into their ability to achieve all that they're capable of.

6. Affiliative Style

"People come first"

The affiliative leadership approach is one where the leader gets up close and personal with people. A leader practicing this style pays attention to and supports the emotional needs of team members. The leader strives to open up a pipeline that connects him or her to the team.

This style is all about encouraging harmony and forming collaborative relationships with teams. It's particularly useful, for example, in smoothing conflicts among team members or reassuring people during times of stress.

7. Laissez-Faire Style

This leadership styles involves the least amount of oversight. On one end, the autocratic style leader stands as firm as a rock on issues, while the laissez-faire leader lets people swim with the current.

On the surface, a laissez-faire leader may appear to trust people to know what to do, but taken to the extreme, an uninvolved leader may end up appearing aloof. While it's beneficial to give people opportunities to spread their wings, with a total lack of direction, people may unwittingly drift in the wrong direction—away from the critical goals of the organization.

This style can work if you're leading highly skilled, experienced employees who are self-starters and motivated. To be most effective with this style, it is necessary to monitor team performance and provide regular feedback.

Choosing Leadership Styles

Knowing which of the leadership styles works best for you is part of being a good leader. Developing a signature style with the ability to stretch into other styles as the situation warrants may help enhance your leadership effectiveness.

1. Understand the different styles.

Get familiar with the repertoire of leadership styles that can work best for a given situation. What new skills do you need to develop?

2. Know yourself.

Start by raising your awareness of your dominant leadership style. You can do this by asking trusted colleagues to describe the strengths of your leadership style. You can also take a leadership style assessment.

3. Practice makes a leader.

Be genuine with any approach you use. Moving from a dominant leadership style to a different one may be challenging at first. Practice the new behaviors until they become natural. In other words, don't use a different leadership style as a "point-and-click" approach. People can smell a fake leadership style a mile away—authenticity rules.

4. Develop your leadership agility.

Traditional leadership styles are still relevant in today's workplace, but they may need to be combined with new approaches in line with how leadership is defined for the 21st century.

Today's business environments are fraught with challenges due to the changing demographics and the employee expectations of a diverse workforce. This may call for a new breed of leader who is an amalgam of most of the leadership styles discussed here.

Leadership theory

Just as there are multiple definitions of leadership, many different leadership theories exist. These theories are often grouped into buckets based on the ideas each theory professes.

For example, one group is the Great Man Theory, a category that originated in the 19th century and stresses that great leaders were men born to the task. Another group is the Trait Theory, which dates to the mid-20th century and also centers on the idea that some people are born with the traits that make them great leaders, such as integrity and self-confidence.

The second half of the 20th century saw the arrival of several more categories. Those include situational leadership, where the leadership style is adjusted based on the readiness or skill level of followers in a given situation, and contingency theories, in which effective leadership depends on having the right leader for the right situation; transactional leadership theories, in which leaders reward or punish followers to achieve results; and transformational leadership.

Principle of path-goal theory of leadership

The path-goal theory states that a leader's behavior is contingent to the satisfaction, motivation and performance of their employees. The manager's job is viewed as guiding workers to choose the best paths to reach both their goals as well as the corporation's goals. The theory argues that leaders will have to engage in different types of leadership behavior depending on the nature and the demands of the situation at hand.

It is the leader's job to assist followers in attaining goals and to provide the direction and support needed to ensure that their goals are compatible with the organization's goals. Path–goal theory assumes that leaders are flexible and that they can change their style, as situations require.

Path goal-theory of leadership

According to Robert J. House (1971), the Path-Goal Theory encapsulates the necessity for distinct roles which a leader must fulfill, as well as the leadership traits managers should acquire in their practice. House also provided guidelines of which leaders must follow to compensate for subordinates' potential skill deficiencies.

Leadership theories

Leadership theories try to examine and study the traits of a leader. In the first theory, the Trait Theory of Leadership, it's believed that leaders share certain inborn personality traits, such as drive, ambition, and self-confidence.

The second learning theory is a behavioral one, where researchers studied the behavioral aspects of effective leaders, such as their ability to motivate people and their communication skills.

The third, contingency theory, advocated that it is the environmental factors surrounding leaders that influenced their ascent to leadership, and that it is not so much their leadership qualities as it is about the situation in which they needed to lead.

Finally, the fourth theory is the transformational leadership theory, which suggests that good leaders are those able to stimulate, transform, and use the values, beliefs, and needs of their followers to accomplish tasks.

Path goal-theory of leadership

According to Robert J. House (1971), the Path-Goal Theory encapsulates the necessity for distinct roles which a leader must fulfill, as well as the leadership traits managers should acquire in their practice. House also provided guidelines of which leaders must follow to compensate for subordinates' potential skill deficiencies.

Leadership theories

Leadership theories try to examine and study the traits of a leader. In the first theory, the Trait Theory of Leadership, it's believed that leaders share certain inborn personality traits, such as drive, ambition, and self-confidence.

The second learning theory is a behavioral one, where researchers studied the behavioral aspects of effective leaders, such as their ability to motivate people and their communication skills.

The third, contingency theory, advocated that it is the environmental factors surrounding leaders that influenced their ascent to leadership, and that it is not so much their leadership qualities as it is about the situation in which they needed to lead.

Finally, the fourth theory is the transformational leadership theory, which suggests that good leaders are those able to stimulate, transform, and use the values, beliefs, and needs of their followers to accomplish tasks.

1. Overcoming Challenges and Obstacles with the Path Goal Theory

Challenges and obstacles are inevitable in the workplace, which is why a strategy must be implemented to avoid and evade these. Providing employees with the necessary tools to resolve issues in the workplace will ensure organizational success is not hindered.

2. Goal Achievement

Effective leadership not only guides employees in the right direction towards their goals but also requires leaders to assist in the identification of goals and objectives from the get-go. Goals should be achievable, meaning that they must be realistic and measurable.

3. Boosted Employee Productivity and Motivation

Effective leaders understand the importance of rewarding and recognizing employees through the offer of incentives and intrinsic motivation. In essence, this is to drive employees to succeed and reach their maximum potential for the benefit of the entire organization. Gamification is a widely-employed strategy by organizations to significantly boost the engagement and information absorption of learners. It encapsulates the implementation of gaming elements into serious course content, such as star bars, point scores, leader boards and real-prizing.

4. Enhanced Support Network

Having a supportive leadership style ensures that interactions remain learner-centered, meaning that employees' personal preferences and emotional needs are accounted for, and are at the center of decision-making. When employees feel respected and valued, they are more likely to develop a stronger bond with the organization and tend to work harder.

5. Increase Employee Confidence with the Path Goal Theory

When employees' confidence levels increase, potential barriers built around their learning are broken down, resulting in them wanting to learn more. The Path-Goal Theory allows for this through the participative leadership approach, whereby once confident, employees control their own personal training path. Increased confidence can be achieved by leaders' constant acknowledgment of employees, praising them on their good work, and providing frequent feedback.

6. A More Functional and Positive Environment

A more positive and functional environment is nurtured when the Path-Goal Theory is applied to leadership training as communication and collaboration allow employees to be involved in daily workplace happenings, making for a peaceful workplace. Having a zen workplace instantly alleviates stress, resulting in employees becoming more productive and being provided with more effective and successful leaders.

Printed by Libri Plureos GmbH in Hamburg,
Germany